Campaigning
For President

A NEW LOOK AT THE
ROAD TO THE WHITE HOUSE

By Marvin R. Weisbord

Public Affairs Press, Washington, D. C.

FOR MY MOTHER AND FATHER

INTRODUCTION

On the surface, the 1964 campaign almost seems a throwback to the days when Grover Cleveland's manager warned him not to make himself "common," and an adviser to William Henry Harrison admonished, "Let no committee, no convention, no town meeting extract from him a single word, about what he thinks now, or what he will do hereafter." Barry Goldwater won the California primary with the second technique. Lyndon Johnson, using the first, seems determined to avoid making himself common.

Despite a public clamor to the contrary, the 1964 campaign is likely to see more face-to-face debate between Huntley and Brinkley than between Goldwater and Johnson. The weight of the past, silent but potent, has held in check every President since Washington. The oldest American tradition requires that a Chief Executive running for re-election should move on padded feet, as aloof and dignified as a Siamese cat.

McKinley, Theodore Roosevelt and Coolidge made no campaign speeches the second time around. Woodrow Wilson made few. Even Hoover in 1932 and Dwight Eisenhower in 1956 proved extremely reluctant to "go to the people." Until Franklin Roosevelt stumped the country to win a second term in 1936 that trick had never been done before. Most Presidents behaved in the American tradition. The only reason Kennedy and Nixon agreed to confront one another in four "joint appearances" in 1960 is that neither man was President. Each thought he had something to gain on television. The candidates broke a precedent of sorts debating in 1960, but not nearly as strong as the one Lyndon Johnson would shatter debating in 1964.

During most of American history candidates for President, especially those already President, believed they should keep quiet and let other people toot their horns. This tradition was eroded only gradually. Lyndon Johnson, as Chief Executive, doesn't have to worry whether he will be accused of being "afraid" to debate. All he needs to do is point out that no President is required to argue his program publicly with the man who wants his job; to do so would compromise the dignity of the office.

So much for the President's campaign behavior as President. As Democratic *candidate*, however, Lyndon Johnson will, of course, be making personal tours, shaking hands along the way, appealing for votes on the "bread-and-butter" issues which have sustained his party since Wilson's day. By contrast, Barry Goldwater's managers say the Senator is relying more on prepared speeches and less on whistle-stopping than any recent GOP candidate. Goldwater dislikes street-corner politicking, informal question-and-answer sessions, and close contact with the voters—especially those hostile to his views. He prefers sympathetic audiences, and his important speeches are likely to be made in front of staunch partisans, and carried to the rest of the country via radio and television.

A campaign lacking debates, with fewer whistle-stops and motorcades, and more relaxed scheduling is going to seem more old-fashioned than any one in recent memory. Kennedy and Nixon exhausted themselves meeting tight deadlines, cramming in dozens of stops and street-corner talks, criss-crossing the nation repeatedly by jet to keep appointments. Nixon, with herioc energy, made good a pledge to campaign in all 50 states. Kennedy, after traveling more miles than Nixon, spoke, the day before election, in five different cities.

Goldwater refuses to schedule himself so tightly; and Johnson, who must continue to run the government even while seeking the chance to keep on running it, isn't likely to try. In 1964 the vice presidential candidates will be carrying much of the burden on the stump, which is exactly what they did in the old days. (Franklin Roosevelt made 1000 speeches running for Vice President in 1920, about three times as many has James M. Cox, whose running-mate he was.)

However, superficial resemblance to the past quickly fades in the glow of the television screen. Both candidates, debating or not, need radio and television. The electronic media give a man instant access to millions of voters without his having to leave town. They also give the voters an illusion of access to the man. There are some who feel Goldwater considers it an advantage to place mechanical barriers between himself and the voters; Johnson evidently sees it as an excellent means of enhancing his image under controlled circumstances. Hence the present campaign—despite its overtones of the past—is also a glimpse into the future. More and more in politics we are being asked to make up our minds mainly on the basis of what we can learn about a candidate while watching him read other people's words, aided by a teleprompter, into a television camera. Perhaps this is not "democracy" the way the Founders envisioned it; but it is a distinct improvement over the old days when candidates were seldom seen or heard.

Throughout much of American history, as I try to show, we Americans picked our Presidents like mail-order goods, sight unseen, and without really knowing much more than what we were told second hand. How come? What kept candidates from campaigning? How does the past affect us today? These are some of the questions I endeavor to answer in the pages that follow.

ACKNOWLEDGMENTS

But for my friend Alden Todd this book would not have been written, and he has put me further in his debt by taking time from his own work to criticize and comment on parts of the manuscript. I'm also grateful for the advice and encouragement of three other friends, Dr. Murray Friedman, George Corbeil, and Bernard L. Segal. Finally, I must thank my father William W. Weisbord for his friendly interest, and my wife and children for their forbearance.

MARVIN R. WEISBORD

Merion Station, Pa.

CONTENTS

Part One

THE CHANGING CAMPAIGN

Chapter 1

FROM LINCOLN TO JOHNSON

"There is a political mystery that needs explaining, especially in an election year. Between the Civil War and the Great Depression the Republican Party was by a wide margin the majority party in the United States. With the country prosperous and in a conservative mood, the Republican Party ought to be the majority party again. It isn't. By a majority of at least five to three, the voters prefer the Democrats. Why?

"There are almost as many answers to that question as there are politicians and political reporters. But it is now time to reveal a startling fact, hitherto unreported, which certainly in part explains the mystery: It is this: *Republicans are more boring than Democrats.*"—Stewart Alsop, in "Affairs of State," *Saturday Evening Post*, April 25, 1964.

"Integrity and firmness are all I can promise," wrote George Washington when the Founders made him the first President of the United States. With becoming modesty he put his pledge into a letter, not a campaign speech. General Washington didn't go campaigning. He didn't have to.

The 1964 aspirants, squaring off for Washington's old job, promised integrity too—also higher wages, lower taxes, more jobs, equal rights, reduced government spending, stronger defenses, cleaner rivers, wider highways, and firmness, yes, but also a much cooler cold war. No one needed to promise the moon. Republican Richard M. Nixon did that in 1960, and the Democrats have been shooting for it ever since.

Washington, in his white wig, kneebreeches, and ruffles would hardly recognize what his descendents, in their conservative dark suits and striped ties, put themselves through today to become President. Jefferson would be equally astounded; so would Madison, the Adamses, Jackson, Pierce, and all the rest clear down to

3

Lincoln. Watching the 1964 aspirants sprint madly from place to place, actively campaigning or just as actively not doing so, it was hard to imagine the paths they trod were not old and hallowed, like the Liberty Bell, Valley Forge and the Spirit of '76.

The tree of liberty has sprouted some fanciful blossoms these last 176 years—a two-party system, nominating conventions, platforms, primary elections—but none more exotic than the campaign for President in which the candidate himself takes part. Imagine an early 18th century hopeful beating a path, as his modern counterpart does, from New Hampshire to Oregon, Wisconsin to West Virginia, from city street corner to village crossroads, shaking hands until his bones ache, surviving for weeks on luncheons of chicken-and-peas, pitching hay with farmers and war-dancing with Indians, kissing babies and beauty queens, complimenting obscure political hacks he will never see again, facing the nation and meeting the press, and announcing his opinions on every matter from Cuba to Vietnam and birth control to unemployment, sleeping four hours a night, smiling incessantly all the while, and wishing he had more time.

If you can't imagine it, you are not alone. The Founding Fathers couldn't either. For more than 100 years neither could most of the men who ran for President. Perhaps "run" is not the right word. In the early days candidates didn't run. They ran away as, indeed, some still do, like peacocks in a rite of courtship. Until this century the United States picked its Presidents largely sight unseen, and, with few exceptions, without hearing from their own lips what they would or would not do if elected.

Not until 1860 did a candidate (Stephen A. Douglas) take a notion to campaign openly for himself. Not until 1912 did a President (Woodrow Wilson) do it successfully. Wilson was the first nominee in history to stump and win. In 1916 he grew more traditional and ran for re-election by making a speech a week from the front porch of his summer home at Shadow Lawn, New Jersey.

It took 20 more years before Franklin D. Roosevelt, swamping Alf Landon in a sea of rear-platform and radio speeches, became the first President to be re-elected after a whistle-stop tour. Only one other had even tried—Herbert Hoover in 1932—and his heart wasn't in it. If President Lyndon Johnson stumps and wins in 1964, he will join a select company which includes, besides FDR, only Harry Truman and Dwight Eisenhower.

This is not to say the presidential campaign was born yesterday. "Issues" aroused the few white American males who could vote as far back as 1800 in Thomas Jefferson's day. By 1840 one could expect torchlight parades, stump speeches and bonfires every fourth year as predictably as locusts every seventh. From the earliest days editors castigated, senators breathed fire, and party managers came out from behind their cigars long enough to make deals. But the candidate kept his mouth shut in public. Shy mumblers like Jefferson or eloquent orators like Henry Clay—all sat out the conflict on the sidelines. A presidential nominee considered it beneath his dignity to chase votes, and the voters whose votes he was chasing agreed with him. This concession to image is perhaps the only aspect of modern candidate behavior that can be traced to the earliest days of the Republic.

How many know that the gaunt, beardless backwoods politician the Republicans put up in 1860 made no campaign speeches? Abraham Lincoln ran for President by staying home in Springfield, Illinois, minding his law practice. He didn't debate Stephen Douglas. He didn't even reply to the unprecedented speeches Douglas, the Democratic candidate, was making all over the country. The two had debated in 1858 during a Senate race in Illinois, which Lincoln lost. In 1860 Douglas had the platform to himself. Lincoln, in fact, thought it reeked of partisanship for a presidential candidate to vote. However, his friends persuaded him to go down and cast a ballot for the other Republicans, which he did— after clipping his own name off the ballot.

By contrast John F. Kennedy a century later came 75,000 miles by jet, train, and motorcade down the road to the White House. His published speeches, press releases and statements made between August 1 and November 7, 1960, occupy more than 1200 pages of solid print. Richard M. Nixon, Kennedy's opponent and Abe Lincoln's political heir, became the first candidate to stump all 50 States. Unlike Lincoln and Douglas, Kennedy and Nixon debated before 100 million people on television—an audience more than three times the population of the United States in 1860.

If voters did not know what their man advocated in 1960, it was not for lack of opportunity. Kennedy with his pointing finger, Nixon with outstretched arms became on TV and in person more familiar than some of one's own cousins. Neither man pretended any Lincolnian shyness on election day. "First order of business," said Nixon, "was to go out to our voting precinct in Whittier so that pictures of us casting our ballots would appear in the afternoon papers, both East and West. Even this bit of publicity might swing a critical vote!"

It is no longer true that the Presidency comes to those who only stand and wait. No modern Washington or Lincoln can expect the job to find him unless he goes out to find it. He must do more. He must convince people he (1) has the ability, self-confidence and judgment to lead the nation the world looks to for leadership; and (2) represents a party which, once in power, will return a little something on the people's investment in the way of growth, prosperity, security, and pride. The parties once did all the work on behalf of their candidates. Today the candidates shoulder most of the burden.

Something happened in politics after 1860 to change radically the campaign behavior of the candidates right down to the present time. The extraordinary trauma of impending Civil War brought Stephen Douglas to the stump; and it's no coincidence that the great stumpers ever since have been, for the most part, like Douglas, Democrats. The Democratic party, as we shall see, invented the modern campaign. The public notification ceremony, the acceptance speech to the convention, the whistle-stop tour, the rear-platform speech, the non-stop handshaking, and the campaign promise were Democratic innovations.

Democrats were no smarter or more imaginative than Republicans. But, as a result of the Civil War, they lost all leverage in national politics. The Democratic party became, after 1860, a once-successful business gone bankrupt. To become solvent again called for unprecedented campaign tactics.

When Lincoln was elected the first GOP President in 1860, the South, solidly Democratic, left the Union. Upon its return a state at a time years later, its dominant party had been decimated. Democrats were labelled members of the Party of Rebellion; it seems miraculous their party survived the war at all. Not only did Federal troops impose carpetbag Republican rule on the South after 1864, but the 15th Amendment gave freed slaves the vote; and they, in gratitude, turned Republican too.

"When Grant entered the White House [1868], the Republican party had become an institution," wrote Eugene Roseboom. "It was no longer a means to an end but an end in itself. It could live on its past. A glorious tradition had been created: the party had saved the Union, struck the chains of bondage from the African, made all men equal under the Constitution and laws, and supplanted a divisive states-rights ideal with the grander conception of American nationalism."

But that wasn't all. Republicans took credit for the transcontinental railroad, completed under Grant. Republicans pushed through the legislation to build ship canals in the West, deepen harbors, build wagon roads—"internal improvements" unalterably opposed by Democrats as federal tampering with states' rights. The GOP gave generous pensions to Union war veterans. GOP policies wedded big business and the "success" idea to Republicanism; the mariage has lasted to this day, although Lyndon Johnson seemed, in 1964, a potential home-wrecker.

Some equilibrium between the parties was restored as a result of the disputed Hayes-Tilden election in 1876. The GOP kept the White House, but when it pulled Federal troops out of the South it paved the way for a Democratic revival. Grover Cleveland, the only Democrat to be President in the long freeze-out from 1860 to 1912, won in part as a result of this new equilibrium. By the time of his second administration in 1892, however, it was hard to tell Cleveland from a Republican.

Around the turn of the century the party of progress, of the forward look, of growth, of reform, the party which businessmen, workers, and even farmers gazed upon with hope was the GOP. Of course there were, as in every age, men who dreamed of a distant idealized past, of a tranquil moment suspended in time and space when life seemed fuller, more satisfying, more certain, and serene. In 1964 they tended to be Republicans; in 1864 they were Democrats. Their slogan, a century ago, went: "The Constitution as it is, the Union as it was, and the Negroes where they are."

In those days the GOP stood for progress; in consequence it held the votes. It won national elections consistently after the Civil War. Yet no Republican candidate for President would deface his image by stumping the countryside. This might do for congressmen or governors, but not a potential President. Washington didn't need to stump; Lincoln wouldn't think of it; no Republican in his right mind was going to rock the boat of tradition. But Democrats, demoralized by the Civil War, haunted by reveries of a time that never was, found the path to the future preempted by Republicanism. Tariffs, trade, trusts, expansion— the crucial issues of the day boiled up out of the GOP. But Democrats were weighty with tradition and an unuseable past summed up in the empty phrase "states' rights." Yet tradition, in the troubled, frustrating years of decline, won them no votes.

So Democratic candidates had little to lose by imitating Douglas rather than Lincoln—except their dignity. And they had lost that already in the Civil War. William Jennings Bryan, the bombastic stumper who was to be a three-time loser, understood the dilemma.

He realized Democrats could not seize the initiative again looking backward. Bryan wrote a formula for the future: "the free and unlimited coinage of silver at 16-1." Bryan's vision required a sharp break with his party's ideological past; but his rear-platform technique grew right out of the Democratic precedent of Stephen Douglas. Stump speaking was for Bryan as natural as eating. Who remembers what the Great Commoner said in the rigorous campaign of 1896? Nobody. But every school-boy knows Bryan was master of the whistle-stop.

So hard did Bryan campaign, in fact, that William McKinley, his GOP opponent, could not remain passive in the parlor. He too coveted headlines and public enthusiasm; but he couldn't risk his precious Republican image. So the front porch campaign, a GOP innovation, was born. By way of the porch Republicans made the journey from the backroom to the rear platform of the campaign train. No Republican could have taken such a long leap all at once.

Even Theodore Roosevelt, of the toothy smile and high-pitched bellow, did not make his bully campaign for President as a Republican. Running for office in 1904 he allowed the GOP to campaign for him. Once elected he refused, in 1908, to make speeches on behalf of his protege William Howard Taft. What makes the first Roosevelt memorable as a great campaigner? The 1912 race, of course, when as a Progressive or "Bull Moose" candidate, he ran against both Taft and Wilson. It took a chronic vote shortage, the classic Democratic disease, to put Teddy Roosevelt on the stump.

Between 1860 and 1932 the less chance a Democrat had of winning the more likely you were to find him out hunting votes. Horace Greeley, Bryan, Judge Alton B. Parker, Wilson, James M. Cox, John W. Davis, Al Smith—these Democrats put the candidate into the campaign. They had to because, like the boy who burned down the barn, it was the only way to make people pay attention.

The GOP, secure in its gilt-edge voting majority, could afford to remain cool, aloof, dignified. The early Republican aspirant had an image to protect; he guarded it assiduously, as a maid her virtue, even if his career up to nomination day had been spent as a party hack ferreting out votes in the wards and precincts. From Lincoln through Grant, Hayes, Garfield, McKinley and Taft, clear down to Harding, Coolidge and Hoover, Republican candidates eschewed stumping. To "grub votes," as they put it, was not dignified. A man of real presidential caliber should be able to win without it. Indeed, the GOP, which had all the votes it needed without grubbing, won consistently.

But even the Yankees have been known to lose a pennant. Sometime between 1900 and 1912 the Republican party suffered a case of arrested development. By 1928 the disease had become chronic, though a rising stock market obscured the symptoms and nobody was ready to call a doctor. Alfred E. Smith, first Catholic candidate for President, lost badly to Herbert Hoover in 1928. But Al Smith did what no Democrat before him had ever done. He captured the votes of immigrants and working people in the big cities. His feat enabled Franklin Roosevelt, in 1932, to put together a winning combination that was good for 30 years.

The Great Depression was the GOP's Civil War. As the Democratic party went up in smoke at Fort Sumter, so the Republicans came crashing down with the stock market. The Party of Depression replaced the Party of Rebellion as the boogy man of Americian politics. The GOP's natural voting majority was shattered by the Depression. Franklin Roosevelt picked up the pieces and fitted together a new coalition which became the new natural home of most voters, as it still is today.

The effect on heretofore lethargic Republican nominees was startling. Alfred Landon in 1936, Wendell Willkie in 1940, and Thomas Dewey in 1944 ran for President like scared rabbits. They broke the tradition of aloofness in the GOP. Inheritors of an irremediable vote shortage, they panted breathlessly after Roosevelt just to stay in the same place. For Roosevelt, in 1932, had 72 years of Democratic campaign tradition to draw upon. The GOP has been a long time catching up.

So GOP presidential nominees have really not been in the campaign business much more than 30 years. Part of the reason "Republicans are more boring than Democrats" (see Stewart Alsop quote at the head of this chapter) is that they still tend to cherish the belief their Presidential nominees should somehow be "above politics." The amateur look is part of the GOP's preoccupation with image, an intangible which, as we shall see in later chapters, seems to stalk the party's nominees to the exclusion of concrete policies that can win.

Republicans, forced almost against their will into putting their nominees on the stump, still strive to elect men (Willkie and Eisenhower) who are truly amateurs, and therefore can get away with anything, to real professionals (Dewey and Nixon) who so cherish the ideal of dignified aloofness their campaigns become exercises in technical subtlety instead of substantive issues. Dewey's 1948 campaign (see Chapter 10) makes a classic case history of a progressive candidate imprisoned in a party memory. This naturally-tough campaigner pulled his punches against Harry Truman because, like Republicans before the turn of the century, he thought he had the election won. He had no intention of muddying the campaign with issues; and Truman, who was not much for images, mopped him up.

Then came 1952. We liked Ike so much we were willing to put the GOP back in the White House to get him. Ike probably could have won running as a Prohibitionist or a Vegetarian. In 1956 he became the only modern President to be re-elected while his party was losing both houses of Congress. For the Democrats retained their natural majority, and, although the Depression recedes further each year into memory, no recent cataclysm has so shaken the party structure as to result in a new line up.

The 1960 Presidential race, as a result, appeared to be more evenly-matched than it really was. Kennedy and Nixon seemed equally hell-bent-for-election; polls showed them running neck and neck. Democrat Kennedy's natural majority was modified by his youth, religion and relative anonymity. Nixon's minority party status seemed greatly enhanced by his close ties to Eisenhower and prominent role on the world stage. Yet Nixon carried a handicap seldom if ever pointed out—the dead weight of recent Republican party history. He became the insecure candidate of a schizoid party torn in two directions, on the left by those who wanted to go back to where Teddy Roosevelt quit and march forward into the future, and on the right by those who wanted to go back to where Cal Coolidge left off and stay there.

The party's recent past offered Nixon no foundation but uncertainty, and perhaps he was nominated because his own personality seemed so like the GOP's. Finding no acceptable guidelines in history, Nixon ended up imitating the only successful Republican in sight—Dwight D. Eisenhower. And the strategy failed him for a simple reason: We liked Ike.

John F. Kennedy, by contrast, had history going for him in 1960 as surely as McKinley in 1896. Kennedy purposely endeavored to run as the spiritual heir of Wilson, Roosevelt and Truman. He acknowledged roots in a substantive tradition, and his campaign had coherence because it linked past and future. It is too simple to say that was the kind of man Kennedy was. More accurately, he was the kind of man his party required. Perhaps the Catholic issue sliced the victory margin thinner than loyal Democrats liked, but it's hard to see how Nixon could have won without making a vastly different campaign.

The chapters that follow try to show that each party by habit and tradition runs its own distinctive kind of campaign for President. The differences in behavior between opposing candidates can't simply be put down to personal quirks. To this day the Republican way of campaigning remains different from the Democratic. Lyndon Johnson could call upon more than his own popularity and political skill in 1964. The shades of Douglas, Bryan,

Wilson, Truman and Kennedy cheered him on. Their records might bolster his own. By contrast, Barry Goldwater faces the handicap of a presidential tradition barren of recent success—unless he can somehow lean upon Dwight Eisenhower, a man many Goldwater Republicans are unwilling to view as an authentic product of the GOP.

Even the campaign promise is largely an invention of Democrats. Woodrow Wilson was the first to make pledges on many different matters a feature of his campaign. In 1960 his political descendent John F. Kennedy set a national record for promising. Commitments tumbled from Kennedy's lips like fruit from a cornucopia. Voters by tens of millions heard him pledge (at LaCrosse, Wisconsin), "If I am elected I will give the farm problem top priority . . ." and (Los Angeles), "I have pledged myself and my party to the immediate enactment of a program of medical care for the aged . . ." and (San Francisco), "I therefore propose a 'peace corps' of the talented young men willing and able to serve their country . . ." and (Milwaukee), ". . . we must establish an arms control research institute . . ." and (Levittown, Pa.), "I pledge myself and my party to seek 80 million jobs by 1982."

Kennedy did not speak for himself alone. He spoke also for his party's past. There were plenty of precedents for his pledges in the programs of Wilson and Roosevelt and Truman, all of whom he cited continually in the campaign. To get to the White House, Will Rogers once observed, candidates "will promise the voters anything from perpetual motion to eternal salvation". The comment is funny, but not wholly accurate. William Jennings Bryan was the last Democrat to specialize in salvation; for 40 years now it has been the exclusive, but not too potent, property of the GOP. Goldwater became its most radical advocate, winning the nomination amid pledges of freedom, moral rectitude and a return to old time religion. Perpetual motion, as Lyndon Johnson demonstrates almost daily, has been the drive wheel of every Democratic campaign since Wilson.

Like so many other campaign innovations, the Democrats evolved the promise when, 50 years after the Civil War, they decided to have done with ante-bellum ideas and face the future. Perhaps simple arithmetic had something to do with it. The Democratic party today includes most of the voters whose ancestors hadn't even come to America when the Civil War was fought. The immigrants, and their decendents, expected a better break in the United States than they'd had in Europe. In the wards of the big Eastern cities they found the local politician, more often than not a Democrat, the man to see for small favors. In return they gave him a big favor: their vote. In time they did more, reshaping the party as they came to help make its policies through their unions and other groups. Unlike the GOP's business constituency, which asked only to be let alone, the Democratic voters made demands— for jobs, shelter, food, and a chance to move up the status ladder.

One can argue a campaign promise is a cheap way of buying votes; oddly enough, in the long pull, most pledges made during a presidential race find some degree of fulfillment. Once a candidate commits himself to something, he is not allowed to forget it if elected. Frequently his conscience goads him as much as his constituents. The man who promises nothing (Harding, Coolidge) usually ends up doing nothing. He who promises more than any man can hope to do (Roosevelt, Kennedy) puts in a busy, and often fruitful, term.

Recently it has been the GOP style to deride promises as "traps to catch votes." This criticism, which Republicans have substituted for real promises of their own, misses the point. For the campaign promise, no matter who makes it, is a mortgage against the future. Like bankers, voters invest in candidates not because they are deceived but because they have hope. The electorate foreclosed on the GOP in 1932 and was tempted to make only one short-term loan on Ike since. Until Republicans can put meat on the bones of their conservative ideology (as the late Senator Robert Taft did), presidential campaigns will operate to Democratic advantage.

Chapter 2

THE RELUCTANT CANDIDATES

"Washington, Sept. 14—The President has impressed upon politicians requesting him to enter the campaign that he does not consider it is dignified for a President of the United States to make political speeches in a campaign. He has followed that course and he recalled to the political managers that the precedent against Presidents making such speeches is strong."—New York *Times,* Sept. 15 1928.

Straight as a gun barrel, the soldier stood on the balcony, gray hair swirling back over his ears. Below a throng of men, women and horses milled in front of "Neill House," best hotel in Columbus, Ohio. Winfield Scott, "Old Fuss and Feathers," conqueror of Mexico City, most notable General since Washington, raised his hand for quiet. It was September 1852, and for three months he had been Whig candidate for President of the United States.

"Fellow citizens," he said, "from my earliest youth, during my whole life, it has been my aim—my ambition—to serve my country as to merit its approbation. I must receive this demonstration as an indication that in some degree my efforts have been successful." The crowd cheered; a few men whistled. Most Ohioans had never seen a presidential candidate. This was a novelty as good as a circus. They turned their faces up, expecting, perhaps, an opinion on immigration, slavery, or Union, three issues much agitating the nation. The General would not oblige.

"My friends," he continued, "I do not intend to speak to you on political topics." Politics, he said, had no bearing on his trip. He was on his way "to select a site in Kentucky, and near Cincinnati, for an Asylum for the worn-out and infirm soldiers. . . " As any newspaper reader knew, Scott had made similar speeches in Pittsburgh, Cleveland and several points between. His was the first deliberate non-campaign on record, and it is notable especially

15

because, unlike the modern non-campaigner (Richard Nixon as he behaved in 1964, for example), Scott was already his party's nominee. He had chosen to violate the taboo against campaiging for himself, or at least to hedge it a little, because he had a problem. In microcosm, it reveals the kinds of pressures from which the modern campaign was to grow.

The General's selection bitterly irked other Whigs, notably Daniel Webster of Massachusetts who felt, reasonably enough, that after a lifetime of public service the nomination belonged to him. Moreover, Scott had endorsed in full his party's platform, including its controversial support for the Fugitive Slave Law.[1] This had alienated Whig abolitionist sympathizers who were out to end slavery. On the other hand, Scott's strong Union sentiments left much to be desired among Southern Whigs. A week after the nomination Henry Clay of Kentucky, the party's founder, died; and Whigs had bolted in all directions.

General Scott, in short, was like a leader without a troop. No manual covered the situation. He had already turned down an invitation to address a rally in honor of the battle of Lundy's Lane (a path of glory he had trod 38 years before), pointing out a political mass meeting was no place for a candidate for President. Still, Scott was a national hero, and his managers, thinking some public exposure might revive interest in his flagging campaign, devised a subterfuge. The General would pick sites for old soliders' homes recently approved by Congress. Campaign or no, he would be seen doing his duty. And seen he was—in Pennsylvania, Ohio and Indiana—as he made it a point not to talk politics on his meandering pilgrimage to Kentucky.

"The fiction that the trip was non-political was carefully preserved," wrote Scott's biographer. "No man was expected, even

---

1. By the terms of this act, passed in 1850, "all good citizens" were required to help catch escaped slaves and return them to their owners. The heavy penalties for helping runaways angered many Northerners, thus exacerbating the bitter feelings that contributed to the Civil War.

after his formal nomination, to solicit openly the people's franchises for the Presidency. The office must seek the man, and an appearance of modest reluctance to admit of sufficient merit for the place had to be maintained."

So General Winfield Scott became the first nominee to put himself where the office of President might find him without much difficulty. It never did. Franklin Pierce, a horse so dark many of the Democratic convention delegates who put him up had never heard of him, stayed home in Concord, kept silent, and rolled up 254 electoral votes to Scott's 42; the General became little more than a footnote to political history.[2] Scott's failure is notable for one reason only. Desperate for votes, fighting to revive a lost cause, he tried to get around an inhibition as old as the Republic. His problem—how to campaign for President without seeming to— bedeviled candidates for decades, and on into the 20th century.

Those who knew no Presidents before Franklin Roosevelt may find it hard to believe that for most of American history candidates for President refused to campaign for themselves. The stump tour, by train, plane and automobile, in which the candidate makes hundreds of speeches and shakes thousands of hands is not ancient ritual, like the inauguration ceremony. This modern campaign constitutes a sharp reversal of an old American tradition, whose origins we will come to shortly.

But first, see how the tradition operated on a whole succession of candidates. Before the Civil War the taboo against campaigning for oneself was so strong some men would not discuss issues even in private. John Frémont, the Republican party's first nominee, for example, had strict orders in 1856 not to talk politics with anybody but his managers. "I called upon him at his home some time before the election," wrote one journalist, "and he was so

---

2. The Democratic campaign slogan deserves a footnote, too. "We Polked you in 1844, we shall Pierce you in 1852!" they declared.

extremely cautious that he evaded the most ordinary expressions relating to the conduct of the battle."

The taboo applied only to candidates for President. Though Frémont wouldn't talk for himself, more than 50 speeches were made in his behalf by a Western Whig-turned-Republican named Abraham Lincoln. Four years later Lincoln, whose father used to find him making mock speeches on tree stumps at age 15, won the GOP nomination himself. What did he do? He pulled the cloak of silence discreetly around his shoulders and, despite the bitterness of the contest, would not campaign. A cartoon of 1860 shows him with padlocked lips.

Pressed to repeat his views on slavery, Lincoln told people to look up his seven debates with Democrat Stephen Douglas, when they had opposed each other for the Senate in 1858. "Those who will not read or heed what I have publicly said would not read or heed a repetition of it," he said in one of the neatest sidesteps in political history. Lincoln's main rival for President, the rambunctious Douglas, became, in fact, the first nominee to solicit openly his own votes. As we shall see, the weight of tradition pushed hard on Douglas. His behavior was called coarse, vulgar and, many felt, beneath the dignity of the office he was seeking.

GOP candidates after Lincoln tended to emulate the Great Emancipator and not his erratic opponent Douglas. Ulysses S. Grant refused to express his views in 1868, managing to conceal behind the facade of aloofness the fact he had none. His Democratic opponent, reluctant Horatio Seymour, made a few speeches in a half-hearted bid for attention that failed. For the most part Democrats were not popular in the years of Reconstruction. General Grant, running again in 1872, declared he would play no role in the campaign. "It has been done, so far as I remember, by but two presidential candidates," he said, "and both of them were public speakers and both were beaten."

Smug in his theory that the best speaker got the fewest votes, Grant left the stage to the idealistic, eccentric Horace Greeley, editor of the New York *Tribune*, the Democratic nominee. Greeley, with his white fringe beard and metal-edged spectacles, was no orator. Yet his candidacy aroused so little support he decided, as many Democrats would, to do a little stumping—in Maine, New York, Pennsylvania and Ohio. He did a creditable job, too, showing people he was more of a good-hearted old man than the ogre of popular fantasy. In these early days many state elections—for governor, state legislature and Congress—were held in advance of the November balloting for President. As Pennsylvania, New York and Indiana went Republican in October, Greeley saw his inevitable defeat coming, and he quit the stump.

The Issues. Though 19th century nominees avoided stumping, this does not mean their views or those of their party could not be discovered. "Issue" politics had developed early in American life—in the conflict between the parties that sprang up around Thomas Jefferson and Alexander Hamilton before 1800. In the next 50 years conventions, platforms, and acceptance letters—none of them envisaged by the Founders—evolved; and any newspaper reader, if he cared enough, could follow the shifting winds of politics.

Conventions and platforms turned out to be remarkably durable in American politics, although there is nothing in the Constitution to suggest they are necessary or even desirable. George Washington, of course, became President without having to run against anybody. From 1800 to 1824 Congressmen from each party met to decide among themselves on suitable candidates. But this method smacked too much of government by secret conclave. Andrew Jackson, the lean son of Tennessee, was proposed for President by his state's legislature; and his candidacy was promoted in a series of meetings around the country.

The first convention was not held until the United States was 45 years old. It was called in 1832 by a short-lived Anti-Mason party, whose members were supposed to have in common a distaste for the secret rituals of Freemasonry. However, the prejudice against Masons was far from universal (even Jackson was one). Though the party had little support outside of New York state, it decided to run a man for President. Its elected Congressmen were few, so to nominate a candidate the Anti-Masons took up an idea Senator Martin Van Buren had proposed in vain to the Democrats five years earlier. They called a convention of delegates at Baltimore. However, they had trouble finding a candidate willing to run. In desperation they turned to an ex-United States Attorney General named William Wirt. Wirt admitted he had been a Mason and saw nothing wrong with it, but the party wasted no time splitting hairs and nominated him. (Some will recall the GOP in 1940 found it no more difficult to put up Wendell Willkie despite his having been a Democrat a few years before.)

As for platforms, the parties got along without them for half a century. Not until 1840 did the Democrats, having met in their first convention, draw up a nine-point statement of principles upon which their candidate, Martin Van Buren, was willing to stake his election. The first platform ran only 700 words, and it was much too abstract to be dramatized on TV.[3] Rather than specific pledges, the Democrats outlined what they believed to be the outer boundaries of Federal government. Their basic tenet was that the central government should spend no money on anything but national defense. Each state, they said, was obliged to preserve its integrity by resisting federal funds for roads, dams, canals, and railways, which were condemned under the general label "internal improvements." Nor would these early Democrats tolerate national banks, federal regulation of slavery, or taxes for anything except "to defray the necessary expenses of government."

The United States government was viewed as a holding operation, not an instrument for solving national problems. The ideo-

---

3. By contrast the 1960 Democratic platform ran nearly 20,000 words, a small book by itself. Short on theory, it detailed specific aims: to curtail Communism, control arms, build world trade, enrich poor nations, create jobs, raise wages, end blight, foster equality, reform the tax structure, etc.

logical roots of Franklin Roosevelt, Harry Truman, John Kennedy, or Lyndon Johnson are nowhere to be found in the first Democratic platform. Instead it contained the seeds for the Goldwater Republicans' family tree—limited spending, low taxes, minimum regulation, states' rights—even though the GOP was still unborn, and its first President, old Abe Lincoln, would not come out of the wilderness for 20 years.

Believing their principles timeless, the early Democrats repeated them verbatim in 1844, 1848, 1852 and 1856, while adding a new issue or two to the basic text. By 1856 the platforms of the newly-founded Republican party and its Democratic rival spelled out in bitter words the conflicting viewpoints of North and South on the future of slavery. Democrats insisted Congress must leave the South's unique labor system alone; the Republicans argued the United States was obliged, under the Constitution, to regulate slavery in the interest of national welfare. The election of a Democratic fence-sitter, James Buchanan, in 1856, postponed the showdown. But in 1860 the conflict shifted—for the only time in American history—from a clash of words to be replaced, at Fort Sumter, Bull Run, and Gettysburg, by a brutal clash of arms. And the Democratic party entered its long winter of decline.

So were sown the seeds of the modern campaign for President.

The two major parties disagreed over more than slavery. From its first platform in 1856 the GOP called for a railroad from coast to coast to be built with federal aid. It also asked Congress to vote money to develop rivers and harbors. Thrust into control of Congress as well as the White House by the Civil War, the Republicans were quick to act on these pledges. The Union Pacific's golden spike was driven at Ogden, Utah, in 1869, joining the Missouri River to the Pacific Ocean in time for President Grant to claim credit for it.[4] The mutual attraction between the GOP and enter-

---

4. Having taken credit for the railroad, he could hardly escape blame for the scandals that attended its building in the form of enormous profits made on government loans with the laying of each mile of track.

prising lumbermen, mine-owners, steel magnates and oil speculators contributed to the rapid growth of the West, of industry, of
some of America's lengendary fortunes, and a few classic scandals.
So the Republican party, bolstered by business support, became
more firmly entrenched than ever. The party's big business power
center survives today, though not by means of the graft, corruption,
plunder, and waste of land, timber, water and Indians now sum-
marized as "the winning of the West."

Once parties started writing platforms, candidates had to make
known their stands on various issues. Since campaigning was out
of the question, the "letter of acceptance" became a device for
clarifying (or in some cases, muddying) one's ideas. In the early
days presidential aspirants stayed away from national conventions.
To attend was to raise the suspicion one was looking for something—the nomination, perhaps. The proper stance was that of
watchful waiting at home in Concord, Springfield, or Canton, while
the managers pulled wires at the convention.

Candidates, then, could not accept the nomination in person as
they do now. They waited home for a committee to come calling,
perhaps weeks later, to "notify" them they had been chosen. The
delegates would be invited into the parlor, served drinks (whiskey,
if they were lucky; water, if, like Mrs. Lincoln, the nominee's
wife detested alcohol). Once notified, the candidate responded
with a short speech of thanks.[5] No one was likely to hear him

---

5. The humor of this charade did not escape contemporary observers. Here is
Lincoln's notification reported, tongue-in-cheek, by an Indiana newspaper: "The Official
Committee arrived in Springfield in dewy evening and went to honest Old Abe's house.
Mrs. Honest Old Abe said Honest Old Abe was out in the woods splitting rails. So the
Official Committee went to the Woods, where sure enough they found Honest Old Abe
splitting rails with his two boys. It was a grand, a magnificent spectacle. There
stood Honest Old Abe in his shirt sleeves, a pair of leather home-made suspenders
holding up a pair of home-made pantaloons, the seat of which was neatly patched. . . .
'Mr. Lincoln, Sir, you've been nominated. Sir, for the Highest office, Sir—' 'Oh don't
bother me,' said Honest Old Abe, 'I took a stent this mornin' to split three million
rails afore night and I don't want to be pestered with no stuff about no conventions till
I get my stent done. I've only got two hundred thousand rails to split before sundown.
I kin do it if you'll let me alone.' "

speak again unless he won. Then, having plenty of time on his hands, he wrote a formal letter accepting the nomination and endorsing, plank by plank, as much of the platform as he thought would bear his weight. The letter, of course, was released to the press.

Theodore Roosevelt, author of a dozen books, big-game hunter, explorer, and politician, raised the acceptance letter to its flowery pinnacle. TR only wrote one, but he wrote it for the ages. He ascended to the Presidency in 1901 after William McKinley had been shot by the anarchist Leon Czolgosz at the Pan-American Exposition in Buffalo. In the GOP tradition, Roosevelt did not campaign when renominated in 1904. Instead, he put his views into a 15,000-word acceptance letter, which was five times longer than his party's platform.

His letter defended Republican policies on every front: domestic and foreign; business, labor, and farm. It restated the well-worn GOP positions on protective tariffs and the gold standard. But it also revealed the emergence of America from its isolation from the rest of the world—a recognition of obligation toward the Philippines, for example, which had been won in the war with Spain. And in it one can sense the effects of the progressive ferment of the 1890's, which had contributed to civil service reform, and the enforcement, cited by TR, of the interstate commerce and anti-trust laws. Even in 1904 the President recognized "the fundamental idea that each man, no matter what his occupation, his race, or his religious belief, is entitled to be treated on his worth as a man and neither favored nor discriminated against because of any accident in his position." And he acknowledged "there is painful difficulty in the effort to realize this idea," a comment of poignant relevance 60 years later.

Once the shifting balance of parties brought nominees to campaign for themselves, the letter lost its point. Franklin Roosevelt, whose 1932 election gave the Democrats their first clear majority since the Civil War, interred the custom for good. He did not wait to be notified but purposely, as we shall see, broke precedent and flew from Albany to Chicago to accept his nomination with a personal speech to the convention. Roosevelt's bold move shattered the tradition that presidential aspirants must avoid conventions lest they come down with a bad case of politics. Today every man who imagines he has an outside chance, can be found hovering near the rostrum at his party's convention, siutable phrases of acceptance dancing, like sugar plums, in his head. Often, just in case, he has the speech written out and tucked in his inside coat pocket, too.

Aloofness. Aside from Douglas' adventure on the eve of Civil War, no Democrat went boldly to the whole country before 1896. The disputed election of 1876, in which Samuel Tilden, a Democrat, won the popular vote, and Rutherford B. Hayes was awarded the office by a single electoral vote, suggested the parties were in balance again. In fact, many voted Democratic that year to protest the Grant scandals. They would return to solid Republicanism soon enough. Part of the deal making Hayes President required him to pull out the last Federal troops from the South, ending carpetbag governments. Southern Democrats soon chased out the Republicans and took away the vote—largely pro-GOP—Congress had recently given Negroes.

Nationally, the Republican party remained dominant. The old tradition of aloofness had been broken by some bold Democrats; but no new campaign tradition emerged before 1896. The campaigns of the 1880's were among the dullest on record. Both parties displayed a hog's greed for patronage and little interest in public welfare. Lord Byrce, America's English friend and observer, noted in 1888 that a candidate's decision to stump in a Presidential election "depends on his popular gifts. If he is a brilliant speaker his services are too valuable to be lost; and he is sent on a tour of the doubtful states . . ."

Probably Byrce did not realize a strong tradition existed against presidential candidates speaking even if, like Henry Clay or Daniel

Webster, they had been the best orators of their day. As late as 1884, Grover Cleveland, a reform Democrat from New York, won the Presidency with only two speeches, despite the revelation he had fathered an illegitimate child. With breathtaking candor Cleveland admitted the charge and was elected anyway, by a hair, over James G. Blaine of Maine. This was the campaign where a Protestant clergyman at a Blaine rally carelessly branded the Democrats the party of "Rum, Romanism, and Rebellion," losing precious Irish Catholic votes in New York for Blaine, who had a right to count on them since his mother was a Roman Catholic and he was of Irish descent.

In 1888 President Cleveland lost to Republican Benjamin Harrison in a close election, but ran again and beat Harrison in 1892. Cleveland was the only Democratic President between Buchanan (1856) and Wilson (1912). Having broken the GOP's grip once, however, the Democrats recognized some bold innovation might tip the scales for them again. William C. Whitney, a Cleveland adviser, suggested the 1892 gimmick—to move the notification ceremony out of the parlor and into the public eye. It should be staged, he said, to publicize Cleveland's ideas, especially on the tariff, which the GOP had made a preeminent issue.

"That it is a wise move there can be no doubt," commented the New York *Herald*, when the plan was announced. A big public ceremony "cannot fail to give the Democratic campaign a 'boost' which will be felt all along the line." That is just what happened. More than 18,000 people came to the first public notification. They heard Cleveland say he opposed the GOP tariff, which protected business and hurt labor, but he would be in a favor of a tariff that protected both.

The Democrats went no further than this innovation. They had no intention of putting Cleveland on the stump in 1892. Some historians have called their decision an act of sportsmanship in deference to President Harrison, whose wife's illness was said to keep him from campaigning. But this view overlooks two facts. First, no President had ever stumped for his own re-election and none would until 1936. Second, the "campaign" Harrison supposedly abandoned was hardly a national tour. It called mainly for a handful of speeches in Cleveland's home territory, New York, which the GOP imagined would be hard to carry. Even these were to be disguised, as were Winfield Scott's, so as not to seem too political. Harrison was to make them enroute to the Capitol from his summer cottage in the Adirondacks. However, when a late summer cholera epidemic struck, the President rushed to his wife's bedside in Washington. Mrs. Harrison died at the end of October, and her husband finished the campaign having made no New York speeches at all.

Cleveland's "sportsmanship" turns out to have been the weight of precedent. Declining an invitation to speak at Chicago, he said, "I am unwilling to make a trip which . . . would be regarded as a political tour made by a candidate for the Presidency." He added that his "general aversion" to the trip was reinforced by the illness of Harrison's wife. But Cleveland was careful to get in his licks in New York state. In late October he spoke to the Buffalonians Cleveland Club (he had been mayor of Buffalo) and a German-American meeting in Manhattan. On November 1 he addressed the Businessmen's Democratic Association of New York City, and, just before election, ran over to Jersey City for one last speech.

During the campaign Cleveland also wrote a number of letters on issues, some of which found their way into the newspapers. This alarmed Whitney, who informed him that the recipients were using his letters "in such a way that it will lose you in a short time that position you have that we talked about when we were considering whether you had better make yourself common in the campaign." This, Whitney, concluded, amounted to overexposure; it was undignified, he reprimanded Cleveland, "to use your ordinary correspondence to familiarize the public with you in a commonplace character . . ."

Whitney's view—and American history flowing back to George Washington supported it—was that the more discreet the candidate, the better. His idea was echoed as recently as 1924 by the sharp-faced Vermont Yankee, Calvin Coolidge, whose opinions H. L. Mencken said "are harmless because they are mainly unknown." The Republican Coolidge made no partisan speeches when, having become President at Warren Harding's death, he ran for re-election in 1924. "I found early in life you don't have to explain something you hadn't said," remarked Silent Cal. In 1928 (see quote that precedes this chapter) President Coolidge, like Theodore Roosevelt in 1908, refused to speak in behalf of his successor Herbert Hoover. To this day many people believe Coolidge's silence merely a quirk of his New England personality. Taciturn he was, but it must be remembered that no incumbent Republican President had ever made more than a half-hearted effort to secure his own re-election. They *all* considered it undignified, even the voluble TR, whom no one ever found at loss for words. Coolidge was right in the tradition.

Until well into this century the idea persisted that Presidents must seem to remain "above politics." Any descent from the heights of dignity to the arena of campaign combat meant a willful, probably fatal, fall from grace. Candidates for Congress might tramp through the mud and rain, grubbing votes where they could find them. But not the candidate for President; for him the dignified acceptance only, then a discreet wait behind the scenes in his home town. Let Vice Presidents, senators, bosses, lesser politicians and amateurs slug it out in his behalf. In 1892 a handsome young Congressman named McKinley, one eye already on the White House, made dozens of speeches from Maine to Minnesota for Benjamin Harrison. Advance exposure was important to the build-up. But when McKinley's turn to run came in 1896, he sat on his front porch and let others take the stump. Every candidate before the Civil War, and most Republicans until 1932, held aloof from campaigning. During most of American history a nominee would no more have thought of openly seeking votes than Al Capone of personally hi-jacking beer trucks.

Why the pose?   When the forces of politics pressing on the
nominee commanded "Go!" what voice inside whispered "Not
yet"?   How could men who had divided their time for years between the backrooms and the platform suddenly become so sensitive
to image with the highest gift of politics at stake?   Who were they
kidding?   Not themselves, certainly, and not the readers of any
daily newspaper.   They seem to have been kidding a ghost.   From
the start, the powdered eminence of George Washington, which
this day looks down in stern dignity from the wall of some first-
grade classroom upon a future President, overshadowed every
aspect of the office.

George Washington's Legacy.   Obscured in the backwash of history, Washington's image once dominated the behavior of every
aspirant to the Presidency.   That's why the Whigs, in their 1848
platform, thought it sufficient to say that if elected Old Rough and
Ready Taylor "will make Washington's Administration the model
of his own."   That's why so many aspirants today, perhaps without
realizing it, pretend they are not interested in being President but
will serve if the people insist.

For no early American wanted less to be President than George
Washington.   He much preferred a gentleman planter's life to the
battlefield or the hurly-burly of politics.   For years he had yearned
for the moment when, his infant country firmly launched, he could
get back to his Mount Vernon farm to spend a tranquil old age.
By 1788 he was tired of public life and felt he had earned a rest.
"So unwilling am I," he wrote in 1789, "in the evening of a life
nearly consumed in public cares, to quit a peaceful abode for an
Ocena of difficulties," for he thought himself "without that com-
petency of political skill, abilities, and inclination which is necessary to manage the helm . . ."   Yet the Founders had given the
office of President unique powers in the expectation only one man
was equal to the job.

Underlying the early debates over what a President should do, wrote Clinton Rossiter, was "the universal assumption that George Washington, the Cincinnatus of the West, would be chosen as first occupant of the office—and chosen and chosen again until claimed by the grave." With this idea in mind, says Rossiter, it is no surprise "that all arguments over the executive at Philadephia were resolved in favor of power and independence." If the President was to be George Washington, power was safe in his hands. (A few even wanted to make the General a military dictator, an idea that appalled him.)

So the office of President sought Washington the way a homing pigeon flies home. Tall, dignified, and an adroit manager of men, the General seemed the only man truly capable of steering this new nation through its stormy infancy. Washington was chosen, not elected. And therein lies the secret of the behavior of the candidates for President who came after.

By modern standards Washington would have made a poor campaigner. Not diffident exactly, he had a natural shyness, a reserve with strangers, that made him seem more cold and aloof than his friends knew him to be. He spoke poorly in public, pausing often and dragging out his sentences; the hearty handshake, the arm-around-the-shoulder, the charming compliments, were remote from his nature. In short, he was no public "personality," and on television he would have been a bust. The Founders showed better sense picking him than their descendants would when, given a choice, they elected—to cite the worst example—Warren Harding over James M. Cox. George Washington, in 1788, spelled "hero," but the word "President" was the label on an empty bottle. Washington filled it with his immense presence, and every candidate since has sought to have a sip.

Yet Washington, not having to campaign for office, left no precedents whatever for the nominees of posterity to follow. His only legacy was the image of aloofness, of reluctant service, of the man who leads not for party, money or glory, but because he loves his country. The image has proved more durable than the substance behind it. Time and again party pros implored Great Generals (never Admirals) to run for President whether they had any interest in politics or not. The reason seems obvious. They were trying, like alchemists, to resurrect George Washington. No wonder the Whigs put up General Winfield Scott instead of the skillful Daniel Webster. No wonder Generals turn up available so often at national conventions. Who could be more above politics than a soldier-hero whose life had been spent in remote Army posts? Who could better convey the Washingtonian image? Who was more likely to win?

Even professional politicians, trying to fill Washington's giant boots, cultivated his image by staying aloof from the campaign. Though parties, conventions, platforms, and acceptance speeches were grafted onto the tree of 1788, the candidate, chief actor in our drama of national politics, held aloof backstage. In this way, 70 years went by during which no nominee would court votes publicly for himself. Then, in 1860, something happened to make Stephen Douglas break abruptly with the American past.

Part Two

BREAKING THE OLD TRADITION

Chapter 3

DEMOCRATIC DEMISE:

STEPHEN A. DOUGLAS

> "It is not personal ambition that has induced me to take the stump this year. I say to you who know me that the presidency has no charms for me. I do not believe that it is my interest as an ambitious man to be President this year if I could. But I do love this Union. There is no sacrifice on earth that I would not make to preserve it."—Stephen A. Douglas, 1860.

Stephen A. Douglas of Illinois, was only in his late 40's in 1860, but he had the lined face of an old campaigner. At the Democratic convention in Charleston, South Carolina, he expected to be nominated for President. Eight of the last eleven Presidents since Jefferson had been Democrats; Douglas pictured himself moving, in the grand tradition, into the White House.

His fantasy was soon shattered. For more than a decade an intra-party war over slavery had been simmering among Democrats. The Southern extremists had fought every attempt by the federal government to determine slavery's future. They insisted on a platform calling for the protection of their "peculiar institution" in territories like Kansas, where a shooting war had broken out over the issue. The South argued it could take that "species of property recognized in fifteen sovereign states" into any territory, federal or local laws to the contrary. The "property" meant slaves.

Douglas took the view—as he had against Lincoln two years before—that slavery "follows the sun." It would go where the cotton grows, and could not be advanced or abolished by law. "I assert that if the people of a territory want slavery, they have a right to have it," Douglas declared, "and if they do not want it, no power on earth should force it upon them." The theory seemed

33

reasonable enough.   Unfortunately, it would not work; its failure brought Stephen Douglas to the stump—the first presidential candidate to solicit his own election.

Douglas had spent most of his adult life in politics, serving as Democratic state chairman in Illinois in 1840, and later as secretary of the state.   Before age 30 he had been elevated to the Illinois supreme court.   Driven by energy and ambition he won a seat in the House of Representatives; by 1845 he was in the United States Senate, and it seemed clear he had his eye on the Presidency.

Douglas figured to win by achieving a modus vivendi between North and South on the slavery issue.   He helped pass the Compromise of 1850, a sectional deal to make California a free state, permit slavery in the new Utah and New Mexico territories, and tighten the Fugitive Slave Law.   Douglas misjudged when he thought the Compromise would gain him the Southern support he needed to be nominated.   In 1852 the dark horse Franklin Pierce slipped in.

Douglas was stubborn.   To court the South he introduced the Kansas-Nebraska Bill in 1854.   The bill passed, making slavery in all sections a matter of local option.   Southerners breathed easier; but Northern abolitionists burned Senator Douglas in effigy. Then Kansas opted for freedom.   This, Douglas thought, should placate the North.   He did not foresee that armed men from Missouri would pour into Kansas to drive anti-slavery voters away from the polls.   Soon two state constitutions, one slave, the other free, touched off a miniature civil war.   It demonstrated the Achilles Heel of Douglas' "popular sovereignty."

One definition of a major political party is "a loose aggregate of mutually-antagonistic factions feeding off each other's votes." An important function of the party platform is to serve as peace pipe among factions, billowing clouds of smoky rhetoric skyward to distract enemies from the dissension below.

The Douglas faction sought to use the Democratic platform as a pacifier in 1860. It offered a minority plank labelling the slave conflict a matter best left to the Supreme Court, whose decisions the Democrats would accept. This artless evasion offered a bridge across the widening chasm between North and South. "We are for principles," replied a Mississippi delegate. "Damn the party!"

The Democrats debated hotly for hours. Pro-slavery Southern-ners applauded the fiery demagogue William L. Yancey, of Ala-bama, for five minutes when he shouted, "Slavery is right and therefore ought to be!" Cooler heads, concerned with holding votes in the Northwest, voted in the Douglas plank. Then delegates from Alabama, Mississippi, South Carolina, Texas, Louisiana, Georgia, Florida, and a scattering of other states, withdrew from the convention. The South had been spoiling for a showdown on slavery; now its sons rejoiced. Salutes of 100 guns were fired at New Orleans and Savannah. In Georgia a handful of delegates who would not withdraw were hung in effigy, their dummies stoned and burned.

For 57 ballots the remaining delegates sweated to nominate a candidate. Douglas could get a majority; but by party rule a nominee needed two-thirds of the convention, and the chair ruled this number included walkouts. In confusion and bitterness the convention adjourned without acting. Douglas received the neces-sary votes two months later, at a new meeting in Baltimore. Mean-time, a group of Southern delegates, joined by supporters of President Buchanan, met and put up their own ticket. It was led by John C. Breckinridge, of Kentucky, then Vice-President of the United States. They quickly adopted a pro-slavery platform.

At Chicago, Republicans had nominated the Illinois rail-splitter, Lincoln, who looked more like a Vice-President when the conven-tion opened but managed to get the votes in two ballots. A fourth group, mainly Southern moderates, had organized a Constitutional Union party and entered John Bell of Tennessee. It would be a four-way race, to be decided, it seemed perfectly clear, between Lincoln and Douglas in the Northern states. The South wanted neither man, but the North had most of the electoral votes. Every observer believed the Democratic party, born of Thomas Jefferson, consolidated by Jackson, was dead; it had "died of Douglas" said an editorial writer. [1]

The break-up of his own party foreshadowed, for Douglas, the impending break-up of the Union. The Lincoln Republicans, with remarkable pragmatism for a party so young, had written a platform with a bone for every dog. They would surely get the broadest support. They called for Kansas statehood and action by Congress to keep territories free; but they also affirmed "the right of each state to order and control its own domestic institution." To Pennsylvania manufacturers a tariff so adjusted "as to encourage the development of the industrial interests of the whole country" sounded protective enough. The Pacific railroad was there, as in 1856. German voters, most of them recent immigrants, found comfort in a plank against changes in the naturalization laws and another calling for land grants to homesteaders. After some struggle, the most militant anti-slavery delegates managed to make the convention accept the statement that "all men are created equal," and have "inalienable rights" by reminding the other delegates the Founders had first used these words in the Declaration of Independence.

While Lincoln sat in Springfield balancing the good effects of this well-rounded platform against the Democratic suicide, Douglas had decided on a bold break with the past. He would make a campaign tour North and South to try to talk some sense into the people who were about to destroy the Union. Perhaps it was too much to expect they would vote for him. But he felt compelled to try to convince them even Lincoln was better than chaos.

It is hard, maybe impossible, to make words reflect the passions

---

1. "One journal," the writer went on, "thinks that it died of the 19th century; another says it died of old age and general imbecility. A very religious journal suggests that it died of a visitation of God—for its manifold sins. A Yankee says 'The Little Giant sot on it, and killed it." A wag insinuates that it tumbled off the platform and broke its neck . . . " (*Weekly Illinois State Journal*, 1860.)

of that bitter time in American history. The present civil rights struggle seems a pale reflection of the antagonism between seccessionists and unionists Douglas sought to mediate. Stephen Douglas did not break the tradition of aloofness lightly; only the most ignorant cynic would say he did it "just to win votes." In a quieter time he surely would have emulated Lincoln, kept silent, and left the political war to his backers. But in 1860 his own Democratic party had grounded on slavery's malevolent rock. If he could not save his party, he could try to save the Union.

"The severe and dignified Washington could not be imagined traveling from state to state, haranguing crowd after crowd, flattering, cajoling, joking, hand-shaking, to win a few votes," wrote one chronicler of the 1860 campaign. "John Adams and Thomas Jefferson were politicians who coveted office, but neither could make a speech. Even Henry Clay prince of canvassers, was silent, when a candidate, except to write a few letters." Yet Douglas spoke everywhere, week after week, for two months, as often as 20 times a day.

The United States had never seen anything like it. Here was this short, coarse, vulgar man—the nickname "Little Giant" certainly did not refer to his manners—soliciting a job once held by the aristocratic Washington. Douglas seemed like a compact Andrew Jackson, born of the barroom, not the parlor. At one society reception in Connecticut he stood, cigar in his teeth, spitting on the floor, while the astonished women tried to keep their gowns from trailing.

Douglas' defection from Washington aloofness seemed beneath contempt. The critics skipped his views, which were moderate enough. What rankled them most was that he had the gall to proclaim them. "Douglas is going about peddling his opinions as a tin man peddles his ware," editorialized the Jonesboro (Ill.) *Gazette.* "The only excuse for him is that as he is a small man, he has a right to be engaged in small business; and small business it is for a candidate for the Presidency to be strolling around the country begging for votes like a town constable." To another Illinois editor Douglas' speeches showed "miserable taste, and utter disregard for the proprieties of his position."

At one point Douglas announced he was going to visit his mother and he worked in several speeches on the way. This touched off a wave of satire. A New Hampshire paper commented that to visit his mother in Western New York state, Douglas "naturally came to New Haven, Guilford, and Hartford on his way, and at the latter place, he was 'betrayed' into a speech. Still bent on his maternal pilgrimage, he goes toward Boston . . . at Worcester, some Judas 'betrayed' him into a speech. At Boston, betrayed again . . ." [2] The ruse smacked of Winfield Scott's inspection tour.

Nevertheless, possessed by a demon more frightening than defeat, Douglas plodded grimly on. Short in stature but long on courage, he spoke for "squatter sovereignty"—free choice for settlers on the slavery question—across the South; and he called for Union at any cost. Douglas said what he believed, not what his audience wanted to hear. At Norfolk, Virginia, a man asked him what he would do, if elected, should the South secede. It is the President's duty, Douglas replied emphatically, to enforce the laws of the United States, "and I, as in duty bound by my oath of fidelity to the Constitution, would do all in my power to aid the government of the United States in maintaining the supremacy of the laws against all resistance to them, come from whatever quarter it might."

Despite the novelty of being the first candidate to openly talk

---

2. Back in Illinois they published this poem:

WHY DID I DOWN TO HARTFORD GO?
'Twas not my squatter self to show;
I went to hunt, I told you so,
  My mother.

             **   *   **

At length I hope I shall thee find,
For thou hast been a useful blind,
That I might often speak my mind,
  My mother.

politics, Douglas insisted he was not canvassing. He recognized one issue only, preservation of the United States. "I did not come here to solicit your votes," he told a Raleigh, North Carolina, audience. "I have nothing to say for myself or my claims personally. I am one of those who think it would not be a favor to me to be made President at this time." He could serve his country as well in the Senate, he said.

From the upper South Douglas carried his message northward, trying by the sound of his booming voice to heal the Union's wounds. He understood the temper of the Southern Democrats, who had been his party colleagues for years. He was sure they meant it when they said they would secede if Lincoln won. When the October elections favored the GOP, Douglas admitted what he had believed all along. "Mr. Lincoln is the next President," he told his secretary sadly. "We must try to save the Union. I will go South." He boarded a Mississippi river steamer for Memphis; and the tail end of the campaign found him in Tennessee, Georgia and Alabama, where eggs were thrown at him as he stood on the platform and threats were made on his life.

He was still making Union speeches the day Lincoln won. Up the Mississippi from New Orleans he went, vocal in defeat, trying to spread a gospel of reconciliation with the new Republican President. He might as well have begged the river to flow north. American history reached a climax in 1860 no man could restrain. In December South Carolina withdrew from the Union. In January, Mississippi, Florida, Alabama, Georgia, and Louisiana followed. Texas seceded February 1. By March 4, Lincoln's inauguration day, the Union had been ripped in two and America's greatest tragedy was unfolding.

War came in April. Douglas, throwing his support behind Lincoln, spoke across the mid-west for the Union cause. The Democratic party's greatest leaders had gone with secession. Only Douglas remained in the North. "There can be no neutrals in this war," he told 10,000 people at Chicago in one of his last speeches, "only patriots—or traitors." A few weeks later, after speaking at Springfield, he contracted typhoid fever—and died June 3, 1861, never to know the outcome of the terrible conflict he had tried—by campaigning for President—to forestall. He was only 48 years old.

Miraculously, the blow of secession did not kill the Democratic party, any more than it killed the Union. But the party's wounds proved serious enough to keep it laid up for years. Democrats after Douglas, seeking to restore their party to health, would emulate the Little Giant on the stump; few would claim a higher purpose. Douglas, to paraphrase Woodrow Wilson, lost in a cause that would one day win. The irony is that Lincoln, the man who won, so dominates American history, Douglas' role is all but forgotten.

In part, perhaps, this is because Douglas, going on the stump, broke a 72-year-old taboo; the coarse, cigar-chewing westerner took awful liberties with the Washingtonian image. His contemporaries could hardly forgive him. He died unredeemed. Nobody realized that in breaking one tradition Douglas had set up another. He had willed his party a legacy that would some day be worth a President's ransom in votes. It's hard to see how the Democrats could have revived their party after the Civil War under the old rules of Presidential campaigning. Douglas hacked a path through the jungle of tradition, and it was still visible when William Jennings Bryan, 36 years later, sought to follow it to the White House.

CHAPTER 4

SILVER TONGUE ON THE STUMP:

WILLIAM JENNINGS BRYAN

"Bryan was fooled by the ballot box. Although it is the best machine yet devised to get at popular opinion of the hour, Bryan never realized what nonsense and confusion can come out of the ballot box; never knew that it was an invention of the devil just before they put him in chains. So Bryan always was listening at the little hole in the top of the box, sedulously convinced that what he heard there was the voice of God."—William Allen White, *Masks in a Pageant*, 1928.

A President, the caustic journalist Ambrose Bierce once wrote, is "The leading figure in a small group of men of whom—and of whom only—it is known that immense numbers of their countrymen did not want any of them for President." Second man in the group would be the "titular leader" of the major party out of power. That is the unofficial title of the losing candidate. No titular leader failed to win the votes of so many Americans more than William Jennings Bryan.

With his high forehead, noble brow, glowing eyes, thick black hair and silver tongue, Bryan held the Democrats enthralled for sixteen years.[1] In this time the party sent him to contest the Presidency with William McKinley in 1896 and 1900, and William Howard Taft in 1908. Bryan was always the dragon and never St. George. He lost more heavily each time.

Yet William Jennings Bryan, who was called "Boy Orator of

---

1. Not surprisingly, Bryan was compared to the Father of his country. "Artists have made much over the resemblance of Bryan to Washington," wrote a biographer. "With a wig properly placed, the resemblance is startling."

the Platte" because he ran for President at 36, invented the modern campaign.   He perfected the whistle-stopper's art—5 million men, women and children saw him on the stump in 1896.   He showed how effective a presidential nominee could be in the role of catalyst for social change.   Bryan was a moving performer, so good in fact he stampeded his own party into nominating him, then roused the complacent GOP from the lethargy induced by a glut of votes.   The ghost of William Jennings Bryan still peeks over the shoulders of candidates in 1964, as they go through motions the Boy Orator pioneered before the turn of the century.

Bryan, unfortunately, wasted his career seeking an issue to snatch elections, like rabbits, from the ballot box. He was such a good magician he fooled the Democrats in 1896; in later years he fooled only himself.   He couldn't tell a panacea from a real program.   With his fancy speeches he spun out dogmas like a spider spinning webs, and remained enmeshed long after his ideas had been cast out by the voters in the pragmatic whirl of American politics.   There is a moral in Bryan's campaigns for Barry Goldwater's supporters, who find their man's rhetoric a heady substitute for the confrontation of problems with programs.   The parallel mustn't be pushed too far.   For Bryan, in his presidential races, helped crystallize the progressive sentiments of his age.

Where Douglas stumped for Union, Bryan was an evangelist preaching one long sermon against "the money power."   Money rent his party in 1896 just as slavery had in 1860.   But the Civil War Democrats had marched stubbornly backward into a non-existent past.   Bryan and his backers managed to grab hold of the coat-tails of the future.   They had seen the pinched faces of farmers and miners in the West and South.   They had diagnosed the ailment as too much control of the American economy in New York by the private bankers.   He grew into a potent symbol, the booming voice of the voiceless; and his presence gave impetus to more effective men—to Teddy Roosevelt's trust busting, for example—and to the GOP's early efforts to ride the groundswell of reform.[2]

In college the oratorical prize was Bryan's varsity letter. He loved to speak, especially on religion and morality. His sophomore essay on "Labor" won him first place in one contest. To the 19th century orator two doors opened on the future, the pulpit or politics. Bryan chose politics, but in every act the evangelistic Protestantism of his forbears marked his career. "I am interested in the science of government," he said years later, "but I am more interested in religion . . . I enjoy making a political speech . . . but I would rather speak on religion than on politics . . . I shall be in the church after I am out of politics." [3]

In 1888 Bryan entered politics campaigning for a Democrat in a Republican district. His candidate lost, and in 1890 Bryan ran for and won the seat himself. He enticed his unwary opponent into 11 debates, and in the final one gave the speechless man a copy of "Gray's Elegy" as part of his summation. Two years later, running for re-election, Bryan groped for an issue. "The people of Nebraska are for free silver and I am for free silver," he said. "I will look up the arguments later."

By 1896 he had looked up the arguments, and became as obsessed with silver as Midas with gold. In it he saw relief from pain, misery, hunger and economic oppression. Those of us raised on price-supported food may find the silver-gold conflict hard to follow. In the 1890's the issue seemed starky real, especially to farmers who had been hit hard by the stock market panic of 1893. Wheat, cotton, corn and hog prices dropped to almost nothing. The silver miners of Nevada and Colorado suffered even more than the farmers. At one point 99 per cent were reported jobless,

---

2. In his famous poem on Bryan, Vachel Lindsay wrote:
   Where is Roosevelt, the young dude cowbody,
   Who hated Bryan, then aped his way?

3. He was, too, as his crude defense of the literal Bible in the Scopes evolution trial proved, just before his death.

which meant quarry operators, train crews, foundry workers lost income, too.

From the Far West the solution to economic chaos seemed perfectly simple. The federal government should buy silver, coin it freely, and support its price at a ratio of 16 ounces to 1 ounce of gold. Inflation would result. Money would be cheap. Silver mines would reopen, farmers would get more for their crops and pay their debts; the whole economy would surge upward.

Hitching this idea to government ownership of railroads (whose arbitrary rates squeezed the profits from wheat and corn), disgruntled farmers formed a Populist (People's) party in 1891. Their platform, radical in its main planks, became the crystal ball in which the two major parties would come to see America's future. The Populists demanded, among other things, a graduated income tax, direct election of United States Senators by the people (instead of the state legislatures), civil service reform, an eight-hour day, a postal savings system, and government-owned telephone and telegraph facilities. Gen. James B. Weaver of Iowa polled more than a million votes for President standing for Populist reforms in 1892.

William Jennings Bryan, listening with his ear to the box, got the message. He subscribed to the peoples' reforms; and his sensitive antennae told him the potent issue was free silver. It was this panacea that a group of Mid-Westerners, led by Governor Altgeld of Illinois, had forced onto the Democratic party at Chicago in the Convention of 1896. Not all Democrats rejoiced at the gift. Eastern bankers and holders of farm mortgages, for example—the moneybags behind President Cleveland's campaigns —were less than exicited by the idea. They did not define prosperity as a smaller return on their investments. Observed from Wall Street the farmers of Illinois, Iowa and Nebraska made unlikely-looking political allies.

The Eastern "gold bugs" stood firm for a gold standard alone, but they appeared to be in the minority in the convention. A platform plank was written supporting the "free and unlimited coinage of silver" at 16-1, and a floor debate was brewing.[4] A minority on the platform committee submitted a substitute plank declaring that free silver would "impair contracts, disturb business, diminish the purchasing power of the wages of labor, and inflict irreparable evils upon our nation's commerce and industry."

To this challenge rose the Boy Orator in defense of his magic metal. "The humblest citizen in all the land, when clad in the armor of a righteous cause, is stronger than all the hosts of error," he humbly informed the delegates. " I come to you in defense of a cause as holy as the cause of liberty—the cause of humanity." Bryan once had worked up a little speech where he referred to the gold standard as a "cross of gold" upon which humanity was being crucified. Now he embellished the theme. Turning to the gold delegates he thundered, "When you come before us and tell us that we are about to disturb your business interests, we reply that you have disturbed *our* business interests by your course."

For wage earners, farmers, miners—all are "businessmen," Bryan said. He aligned himself with Jackson and Jefferson; he insisted no other reforms were posible without free silver, that if farmers were destroyed (and here Herbert Hoover would echo him against FDR years later) "grass will grow in the streets of every city in the country." Bryan, pacing back and forth, tossed his thick mane. "It is the issue of 1776 over again," he roared, nearing the histrionic finish, which would carve for him a silver niche in the American legend.

"Having behind us the producing masses of this nation and the world," Bryan rumbled, "supported by the commercial interests, the laboring interests, and the toilers everywhere, we will answer their demand for a gold standard by saying to them: You shall

---

4. Republicans had already been through this mill at their own convention a few weeks before; Silver Republicans had bolted and gone to Chicago seeking better treatment. One of them, Senator Teller, of Colorado, a founder of the GOP, was even mentioned as a possible Democratic candidate!

not press down upon the brow of labor this crown of thorns, you shall not crucify mankind upon a cross of gold!"

When Bryan finished, the audience, in the words of one observer, "went perfectly crazy." Men stamped their feet, whistled, tossed their coats in the air. "I could understand the scenes of the first French Revolution then," recalled the lawyer Frederic R. Coudert years later. "I could understand Mirabeau . . . When I saw what one individual could do to a crowd—a crowd that had been absolutely amorphous, chaotic, individualistic, absolutely unruly, became mono-maniacally fastened upon one man. He must be taken to the sky! I never forgot it!"

The Populist feelings and frustrations of two decades had boiled up and erupted from the silver throat of William Jennings Bryan. He was nominated on the fifth ballot, and his silver plank carried easily; But President Cleveland's group sat unmoved. "Left Chicago," one New Yorker wrote in his diary. "The platform had been announced and there was nothing more to be done—no respectable man could afford to remain." The New York *Times* called Bryan's speech the work of the "gifted blatherskite from Nebraska," proving that "oratory is more potent than reason."

The more disenchanted Eastern Democrats withdrew from the party and put a National Democratic ticket (purest gold) in the field with President Cleveland's blessing. Even party men who decided to stick could work up no enthusiasm for the canvass. "I am still a Democrat," said New York leader David B. Hill, but he added sourly, "very still."

Aside from the miners, Bryan could count only on Southern and Mid-Western farmers for votes. He imagined factory workers in Chicago, Pittsburgh, and Philadelphia might enlist for free silver, but with the Eastern Democrats alienated, there was nobody to sign them up. The Great Commoner, naturally enough, undertook to do it himself. It was a job he came well equipped for by inclination and training.

Bryan's voice, a Stradivarius among political instruments, was his greatest asset. Described as bell-like, booming, musical, stentorian, sonorous, and majestic by those who heard, it, that voice set up sympathetic vibrations upon American heart-strings. It impressed by its tone and power, concealing in a cascade of oratorical flourish the poverty of its owner's ideas.

Bryan had talked his way into the nomination; now, with his divided party facing a healthy GOP, he proposed to talk his way into the White House. Precedents meant nothing to Bryan. Free silver, he believed, would redeem the Democrats; a man need not be shy if his cause is righteous. For a starter he rented Madison Square Garden in New York for his notification ceremony.

"In ordinary times," he told the folks gathered at the Rock Island station to see him off for the East, "I would have desired to have had the notification take place at my home." But this was no ordinary campaign. Principles must rise above personal wishes; and so "I have expressed a desire to be notified in New York, in order that our cause might be presented first in the heart of what now seems to be the enemy's country . . ."

The choice was dictated more by need than principle. New York, with its large electoral vote, was Cleveland's home base, and the local Democrats had written off Bryan. The Commoner believed favorable publicity would attend his debut in the Garden. He would reach beyond the bankers to the people. Despite his virtuosity at improvising speeches, Bryan wrote his acceptance out word for word. The ideas, he thought, must be brief, lucidly stated, and available in advance text for the press. "I concluded that it was the part of wisdom to disappoint the few thousands who would be in the hall," Bryan recalled, "in order to reach the hundreds of thousands who would read it in print."

The decision was a mistake. At the Garden, looking frequently at his manuscript, the Commoner went over like Rachmaninoff playing Rachmaninoff from sheet music. Not only did the Eastern audience go away unhappy, the press announced Bryan's failure in news columns where everyone could see; relatively few people took the trouble to read the full speech. Nonetheless the Democratic candidate, lance in hand, rode out to tilt with the money power on behalf of the Common Man. "This is no small contest," he said. "We have arrayed on either side the great forces of society."

A Brooklyn minister saw things somewhat differently. "I must be heard and will be heard against all dishonesty and anarchy and kindred evil," said the Rev. Cortland Myers about the Bryan campaign. "I love every stripe and star of Old Glory, and it is at this moment in danger. I must speak every Sunday from now until November. I shall denounce the Chicago platform; that platform was made in hell!"

If the Reverend spoke each Sunday, Bryan, scrupulously observing the Sabbath, was active the other six days of the week. From September 9 to November 3, 1896, he sermonized for free silver at the rate of 100,000 words a day. By his own careful logbook, he traveled more than 18,000 miles on four tours, speaking some 600 times, which is still a record (about 200 to 300 speeches is par today). From Nebraska across Iowa, Illinois, Indiana, Ohio and Pennsylvania went Bryan. Up the Hudson to Albany, back to Chicago again, into Wisconsin, and again to New York—by Labor Day he had gone almost 4000 miles by train and, on occasion, ferry boat.

At Yale University he made a faux pas that cost him his dignity and perhaps a few votes too. Wearing a wide-brim black felt hat, black string tie, white shirt, and Prince Albert coat, Bryan stood on a makeshift platform made of saw-horses with planks laid across. Behind him, in black top hats, sat members of the Democratic city committee of New Haven. As Bryan opened his mouth to speak, the students let out a loud Yale cheer, and ended by shouting: "McKinley!" The second time Bryan shook his fist and said something to the effect that he had come from the West especially "to talk to young men who were spending the ill-gotten gains of their parents."

"My papa's honest!" came a male voice in loud falsetto from

the crowd. At that, yells, cheers, shouts and catcalls drowned out the speaker. The crowd surged around the platform. Suddenly a saw horse collapsed; Bryan, waving his arms, plunged to the ground, and the city committee, holding onto their hats, joined him.[5] Later, he attributed the incident "more to youthful exuberance than any intention to interefere with free speech." Going on to Boston, Bryan spoke to the largest crowd in the memory of reporters— estimates ranged from 50,000 to 100,000.

The Commoner seemed to be everywhere. One week found him in Kansas City, the next in Louisville, or Asheville, the following week in Minneapolis and St. Paul. He covered thoroughly the East, Mid-West and Upper South, though he never went further West than his native Nebraska.[6]

Bryan's oratorical skill never failed him. He could tailor a speech to fit the time and place better than any politician of his day. Always he managed to plug into his favorite theme. "They say that here George Washington once threw a silver dollar across the river," he said at the Mary Washington Monument, near Fredericksburg, Virginia. "But remember, my friends, that when he threw that Silver dollar across the river it fell and remained on American soil."

Today, Bryan said, building to the punch line, "We have financiers who have been able to throw gold dollars all the way across the Atlantic, and then bring them back by an issue of bonds . . . Would you believe, my friends, that a silver dollar which was good enough to be handled by the father of his country is so mean a thing as to excite the contempt of many of our so-called financiers?" From the crowd a man's voice yelled, "Bryan, I'm not

---

5. This is the way James W. Wadsworth, Jr., recalled the incident. A New York *Journal* report quoted Bryan saying, "I am not speaking now to the sons who are sent to college on the proceeds of ill-gotten gains." Wadsworth, later a Senator and Congressman (Republican) from New York, was reprimanded as one of the demonstration's ring-leaders. "That," he said, "was my first experience in politics."

6. One great irony is that the states in which he spent most of his time voted solidly Republican. He knew which votes he needed, but couldn't deliver them.

a Christian, but I am praying for you."

That was the effect Bryan's free silver message had on people disposed to believe it. His talk washed the crowds as heavenly rain, for it had nothing to do with politics. He was speaking about the big rock candy mountain, built on a silver base. Bryan knew no more economics or sociology than the King of Siam, but he had matchless skill as a speaker, and free silver was his obsession. "It was the only time in the history of the Republic," commented Richard Hofstadter, "when a candidate ran for the presidency on the strength of a monomania."

Bryan attacked the gold standard like a preacher surveying the evils of hell. "Of all the instrumentalities which have been conceived by the mind of man for transferring the bread which one man earns to another man who does not earn it," he would intone, "I believe the gold standard is the greatest." Omitting local color, one Bryan speech read like the next. His message never varied. "The free coinage of silver is the first step toward the restoration of just conditions in this country," he said at Baltimore. "It will help restore the heritage that has been bartered away . . . When the government has been taken out of the hands of the syndicates, the stock exchanges and the 'combinations of money-grabbers in this country and Europe,' the door will be open for a progress which will carry civilization up to higher ground."

That was the kernel of Bryanism. No problem of mankind was too remote, obscure or complex to respond to the healing balm of silver coined at 16 to 1. Al Smith, who as a young man admired Bryan, said later he was sure The Commoner "talked over the heads of the people." Wrote Smith, "I would be willing to venture the suggestion that not one in ten thousand voters, or maybe one in fifty thousand voters in New York understood what he meant by the coinage of silver at the ratio of sixteen to one." [7]

7. Yet Bryan was always being handed bouquets of chrysanthemums, in the ratio 16 whites to 1 yellow; once he was pulled through town in a carriage by 16 white horses and 1 yellow one.

Nevertheless Bryan plodded relentlessly onward, speaking at every whistle-stop where he could gather a handful of people. His energy was astonishing. He could get along on as little as three hours sleep a night; but, like Teddy Roosevelt, he also had the ability to doze off in an instant, anywhere. "Three minutes' sleep on a bench here, three more minutes in a hotel lobby, half an hour curled up in a day coach," said one observer of Bryan, "and before the twenty-four hours were up he would have had, in one way or another, eight hours."

To remove the profuse sweat he worked up while evangelizing for silver, he would keep a bottle of gin handy and rub himself with it between whistlestops. "He frequently appeared smelling like a wrecked distillery," an historian of prohibition wrote; but no one could accuse Bryan of imbibing; on the train, he pointedly lectured the reporters on the joys of temperance. His singlemindedness on money aside, Bryan made important discoveries about campaign technique which Wlison, Roosevelt, Truman, and even Eisenhower would adopt. Experience soon taught him, he wrote, that "it was necessary to stand upon the rear platform of the last car in order to avoid the danger to those who crowded about the train. I also found that it was much easier to speak from the platform of the car than to go to a stand, no matter how close. Much valuable time was wasted by going even a short distance, because in passing through a crowd it was always necessary to do more or less of handshaking, and this occupied time." By speaking from the car, he pointed out, one also avoided the danger a plaform might collapse; this, said Bryan, he feared more than physical collapse from overwork.

The Commoner also worried about his legendary larynx. He used cold and hot compresses, cough medicines, and gargles to keep his throat in working order. At the end, he wrote, he gave up all remedies and "found my voice in better condition during the latter days, without treatment, than it was earlier in the campaign."

Despite his unique canvass, Bryan received only 6.4 million

votes to the porch-sitting McKinley's 7 million, 176 electoral voters to 271. His natural market—the farmers and miners of the South and West—came through for him. These were precisely the people among whom he had done the least campaigning. The energetic stumping across the Mid-West, through the East, and in New England brought him large crowds, vivid memories, and few votes. He did not win one state north of the Ohio river. Where the farmers were better off—in Ohio, Indiana, Illinois, Wisconsin, and Minnesota—they voted for McKinley.

But the factory workers disillusioned him most of all; they voted Republican too. Bryan had tried to add apples and oranges to get silver, never dreaming they might come up gold. His grand delusion was that he could weld a coalition between farm and factory with his powerful voice. In this regard, he overestimated his talent. No amount of oratory could alter the common-sense economics Bryan, blinded by his own words, could not see.

It is popularly believed McKinley won labor's vote in 1896 because factory owners coerced their men into going Republican. The evidence of pressure on labor is convincing. Some businessmen posted notices saying employees should not bother to come to work the day after election if Bryan won; companies placed orders contingent on McKinley's election. [8] To assume this is the only reason Northern labor went for the GOP, however, is to forget perhaps labor would have gone for the GOP anyway. Bryan never stopped to ask why a wage earner making $5 a week in a mill should have anything in common with a farmer up to his ears in mortgages and sweating out the market price of wheat. He assumed they were all "businessmen" of sorts; but the mill hand can

---

8. Here is a front page story from the Wilmington (Del.) *Morning News*, November 3, 1896: "The Harlan and Hollingsworth Company, of this city, have received a contract for a boat costing $300,000. One clause in the contract provides that in the event of Bryan's election the contract shall be cancelled. If the boat is built here $160,000 of its cost would be paid to Wilmington workmen for wages. The Corporation wanting the boat feel that it would not be justified in having it construced if Bryan should become President."

be excused for not understanding what coining silver at 16 to 1 would do for him.

Bryan never understood it either, even when gold became more plentiful by 1898, providing the inflation for which the Populist miners and farmers yearned. The Commoner, like a spoiled child, insisted the Democrats give him another silver plank to run on in 1900. He said he would rather lose than give up his silver convictions. In fact, he did both; for the real issue of the campaign became "imperialism," which, to Bryan, meant America's acquisition of the Philippines after the war with Spain. He sermonized on this subject as before, but stirred litle enthusiasm. The Gold Democrats avoided him again in 1900, and even the farmers deserted him.[9]

In 1904 the Democrats put Bryan out to pasture, so they thought, and ran a conservative Easterner, Judge Alton B. Parker; but Parker fell before Teddy Roosevelt's strident liberalism; and the party went back to Bryan in 1908 like a reformed alcoholic falling off the wagon. The Great Commoner made his last stump tour on issues the Republicans had pretty much stolen away: tariffs; the trusts; currency reform. At the last the Boy Orator, speaking as often as 39 times in a day, was no more than a middle-aged campaigner quoting the Bible and shouting a familiar "me too." So William Howard Taft, portly, mustachioed, conservative, became President in 1908, and William Jennings Bryan went back to the Chataqua lecture circuit to discuss religion.

For all Bryan's bluster and shallowness (Irving Stone called him "a doughnut dunker in the coffee of other men's ideas") he backed, in his later years, many causes Americans wanted more than free silver; for the Populist ideas—first outlined in the third party's platform in 1892—were taken over by the Democrats, the Republicans, and the Progressives. They entered the mainstream of American life largely through Bryan's work. In 1925, editing

---

9. Bryan's 1900 running-mate was Adlai E. Stevenson, of Illinois, a former vice president under Cleveland. In 1900 a new grandson had just been named after him.

her husband's memoirs, Mary Baird Bryan made an impressive list of reforms the Commoner had backed and lived to see enacted into law. Among them: the federal income tax; popular election of U.S. Senators; publicity for campaign contributions; women suffrage; a Department of Labor; railroad regulation; currency reform; the use of initiative and referendum in the states.

Bryan's thinking may have been fuzzy, but his instincts were good. Seeking needs to resound in the ballot box, he added a modern dimension to presidential campaigning. He put the candidate on public display as a creator and shaper of issues, not just the passive recipient of his manager's political judgments. From 1896 to 1912 Bryan influenced the course of four Republican Administrations. It was the last creative fling the GOP was to have in American politics for a long time. Roosevelt, who proved in 1912 how much Bryan had taught him about campaigning, was rejected by his party. The Progressive movement which Bryan championed and the GOP put on the national stage, fell into Democratic hands in 1912. Its inheritor was Woodrow Wilson, a man who would take Bryan's techniques and apply them to a coherent program of public business. Bryan broke the Democrats' habit of looking fondly backward to the tranquil days before the Civil War. Wilson was to lay the foundations for modern America.

CHAPTER 5

Ph.D. IN POLITICS:
WOODROW WILSON

"I pity the man who in the year 1912 promises the people
of the United States anything that he cannot give them."
—Woodrow Wilson, September 19, 1912.

In 1909 Woodrow Wilson was a college president. In 1912 he
became President of the United States. No candidate since Grant
had come so far so fast. Wilson was the only Ph.D. (not honorary)
ever to be President, and the first chief executive to win the office by
stumping. Naturally enough he was a Democrat. The whistlestop
campaign was a Democratic property clear up to 1928.

Wilson made his bid at a fortunate moment. For 10 years the
hot winds of reform had blown on the landscape, fanned by liberal
Republicans, Populists, Socialists, and Bryan Democrats. Theodore Roosevelt, GOP President from 1901 to 1908, made a reputation breaking up business monopolies; even the cautious William
Howard Taft did some trust-busting, though his conservatism soon
alienated many influential Republicans. Wilson struck for the
White House at the exact moment the GOP chose to stand pat with
Taft in a surging sea instead of trying to ride the progressive tide
in with Roosevelt. (The effect of this rupture can still be observed
in the tug-of-war between Goldwater and Rockefeller.)

Nominated by the party of two precedent-breakers, Douglas and
Bryan, Wilson added another dimension to an emerging Democratic tradition. He set a standard for enlightened campaign oratory against which candidates are still measured. For Wilson was
the only President whose career had been spent neither in the Army
nor in politics. The university was his milieu, where he studied,
taught, and wrote history and political science. In 1912 the nation

55

became his classroom. In a remarkable whistle-stop campaign he
gave lucid, coherent and sometimes inspiring lectures from coast
to coast on national goals. No man running for President had ever
done that before. His performance grew naturally out of his own
background, and his party's and it laid the groundwork for spectacular Democratic campaigns to come.

Wilson's lifetime spanned two catastrophic wars. "My earliest
recollection," he said, "is of standing at my father's gateway . . .
when I was four years old, and hearing someone pass and say that
Mr. Lincoln was elected and there was to be war." Born in
Georgia, young Wilson studied law, gave it up, and went into college teaching. He took his doctorate at Johns Hopkins, in Baltimore, and by 1890 had settled down to a professor's life at Princeton. His attractive lecture style made him one of the university's
most popular teachers. He talked precisely, with humor (he
liked puns), and displayed a talent for drawing analogies from history to current events. Sometimes, when class ended, his students
broke into spontaneous applause.

By 1902 Wilson was President of Princeton; and in 1910 his
interest in politics, expressed until now as scholarship, thrust him
into public life. He ran for and won the governorship of New
Jersey on a throw-the-rascals-out plaform. The rascals in his own
Democratic party thought he would be an easy touch, but Wilson
fooled them. "Promises are made to be kept," he said jockeying
the state legislature into passing a number of laws he had pledged
during the campaign. Across the country the ex-professor was frequently named as the kind of governor who would make a good
President.

With his sensitive face, grey eyes, and steel-rimmed pince-nez,
Wilson looked more in character at a faculty meeting than a party
caucus. But he knew how to play the game. Bargaining shrewdly
with the Bryan faction, he beat the popular congressman Champ
Clark, of Missouri, for the nomination in 1912. It was a good

year for Democrats. A wide chasm between Taft and Roosevelt had hopelesly divided the GOP votes.

The Republicans had seemed in fine shape when TR, retiring as President in 1909, blessed Taft and sailed off to hunt lions in Africa. He was sure his successor would carry out his policies, which, said the dry-witted Senator Dolliver, Taft did, "on a shutter!" Roosevelt, alarmed at reports of reaction in the GOP, hurried home and declared, contrary to his pledge of 1904, he was available for the Presidency. [1]

At the convention in Chicago, Taft conservatives blocked the seating of Roosevelt delegates; and, as observers in the galleries whistled, "Toot, Toot!" in imitation of a steam-roller, Taft was swept into the nomination. Roosevelt was furious. Feeling, he said, like a "Bull Moose," he led a stampede of liberal Republicans out of the hall to form a new Progressive party. One newspaper, the Marion (Ohio) *Star,* called Roosevelt another Benedict Arnold, worse than Aaron Burr, "utterly without conscience and truth, and the greatest faker of all time." Its editor was a rising star of Republicanism, who had been chosen to make the nominating speech for Taft. His name was Warren Harding.

The Bull Moosers were a short-lived but colorful band of idealists, artists, reformers, and intellectuals who rallied behind TR hoping to keep the GOP on the path to the future. Their spirit was symbolized by the Republican editor William Allen White's comment, "Roosevelt bit me, and I went mad." The Progressive platform of 1912, like the Populists' of 1892, influenced America all out of proportion to the party's strength. (It called for woman suffrage, registration of lobbyists, court reform, a national health service, and parcel post among many other things.) The United States in 1912 was in a reforming mood; the only question was

---

1. After his election, TR had said "under no circumstances" would he be a candidate again for a third term. In 1912 he explained that what he meant, of course, was "a third consecutive term." Once out of office for four years, he explained, he was just a private citizen like anybody else.

whether it would be Wilson's style, or Roosevelt's. "I think I might as well give up so far as being a candidate," Taft wrote his wife. "There are so many people in the country who don't like me." On that pathetic note, the President made his acceptance speech and practically dropped out of contention.

Roosevelt, by contrast, threw himself into the campaign with all of the energy he had once expended to charge up San Juan Hill. He was no longer a Republican constricted by the tight bands of party aloofness. In 1904, when the GOP had had a natural voting majority, TR considered it beneath his dignity to campaign for re-election. Eight years later he set the notion aside; he was in the same situation as the Democratic candidate—a nominee scrambling for every vote. "I stand for the Square Deal," said Roosevelt, kicking off his campaign. "I mean not merely that I stand for fair play under the present rules of the game, but that I stand for having those rules changed as to work for a more substantial equality of opportunity and of reward for equally good service."

Wilson, despite a party ancestry traced to Douglas, despite the great Bryan campaigns of recent memory, did not go joyously on the stump. The haranguing of crowds he considered undignified; and though he spoke well, he knew he lacked The Commoner's hypnotic talents and could not hope to match Roosevelt's stamina and cowboy enthusiasm. He would make no campaign tour, Wilson said; he especially disliked the idea of speaking from the rear platforms of trains.

After his nomination, he boarded the yacht of Cleveland H. Dodge, a heavy campaign contributor, with a copy of the Democratic platform and a scrapbook of newspaper clippings. One, a New York *World* editorial, particularly annoyed him. It was headlined: "Planks To Be Broken." On the yacht he wrote his acceptance speech in shorthand—he had no speech writers—approving every plank but two (a single term for Presidents and exemption of American ships from Panama canal tolls). He strongly endorsed planks opposing business monopoly, and advocating downward tariff revision, laws for safety at sea, farm loans, flood control, and regulation of railroads, telegraph, and telephone by the ICC. [2]

In his acceptance Wilson said the platform "is meant to show that we know what the Nation is thinking about, what it is most concerned about, what it wishes corrected, and what it desires to see attained . . ." This was a political scientist's definition, not a politician's. Later, backed by a certificate of election, he would present the bill to a startled Congress, including some politicians not used to taking such talk seriously.

Though Wilson, like Bryan, read his acceptance speech from manuscript, he told reporters afterwards, "The rest of my speeches will be delivered as I like to deliver a speech—right out of my mind just as it is working at the time." Generally Wilson spoke from notes, never more than a page of them. He had a gift for thinking on his feet; and though he repeated the same themes often, his words always came out fresh, inventive, spontaneous—just as they had in the classroom. It was a talent he would soon find more use for than he intended.

Wilson's impulse was to confine his speaking to the large, doubtful states like New York and Pennsylvania. "I intend to discuss principles and not men," he said, "and I will make speeches only in such debatable states where I accept invitations from the party leaders." With this in mind, he opened the campaign with three talks in New Jersey, then retired to his summer cottage at Sea Girt to make further plans. He said he hoped Bryan would stump for him. Of his own part he wasn't sure.

Late in August a noted Boston lawyer visited Sea Girt and changed Wilson's plans. Louis Brandeis, who would be called an "egghead" today, was an expert on railroad regulation and the law of monopoly. Over a long lunch Brandeis helped Wilson clarify his hazy thoughts about how much freedom businessmen

---

2. Constitutional amendments for an income tax and direct election of senators—from the Bryan days—had already come to fruition, under the Republicans.

should enjoy. The lawyer, said Wilson's biographer Arthur S.
Link, "converted Wilson to the proposition that he make his
campaign upon the issue of the restoration of competition and free
enterprise by means of regulation and control of competition itself."[3]

Brandeis outlined a series of steps by which businessmen could
be made to compete with each other. This plan called for breaking
up monopoly industries into smaller companies. It would seek to
prevent such mergers as the swallowing of the Carnegie company by
United States Steel. It contrasted sharply with Teddy Roosevelt's
idea. TR believed business monopolies were as inevitable as death
and taxes. All the government could hope to do is regulate them
"in the public interest." He did not propose to break them up.

Brandeis gave Wilson the campaign theme he needed to justify
a whistlestop tour. Political platitudes on justice, prosperity and
freedom, Wilson felt, were a waste of his own time, and the people's. But an educational tour was something more. The professor gave up his plan to stay remote unless asked to speak. In
September he began the first of three campaign swings to the Mid-
West, New England, and the East.

Wilson's first speeches revealed his natural shyness with strangers; the stump was not a classroom where the teacher could unbend
a little as he got to know his students. Each day—sometimes many
times a day—there was a new audience to address. Wilson tried
putting his arguments into a few words. "A trust is an arrange
ment to get rid of competition and a big business is a business that
has survived competition by conquering in the field of intelligence
and economy," he would say. "I am for big business and I am
against the trusts." Then the rain would start up, and he would be
left wanting to explain exeactly what he meant. A few days later,
in Indiana, Wilson stopped talking about trusts in his 5 minute
stops. "I have tried discussing the big question of this campaign

---

3. Wilson later appointed Brandeis to the Supreme Court.

from the rear end of a train," he told a knot of people gathered in the roadbed at Michigan City. "It can't be done . . . By the time you get started and begin to explain yourself the train moves off. I would a great deal rather make your acquaintance than leave a compound fracture of an idea behind me." And the professor reached across the rail and began shaking hands.

After that he went into detail only in his major addresses. Soon he caught the rhythm of the stump—small talk at frequent whistle-tops, long speeches to clarify the big issues. On October 3, at the Washington Baseball Park in Indianapolis, Wilson moved into high gear. The Republican party is split, he told an immense crowd, but there's no difference between the halves. Monopolies grew under Taft and Rosevelt both. The job was to break up the trusts, not regulate them. Let businessmen compete freely with one another in the marketplace without government interference. Then, speaking of himself in the third person, he said, "I tell you frankly, I am not interested even in the person who is the Democratic candidate for President . . . I am sorry for him because I believe he is going to be elected . . . And there will be no greater burden in our generation than to organize the forces of liberty in our time, in order to make conquest of a new freedom for America."

"New Freedom"—that was the slogan. It described exactly, Wilson felt, the idea Brandeis had in mind. The more often Wilson talked about it the more confident he became. Soon the stern schoolmaster began to relax on the stump. Never an enthusiastic backslapper or handshaker, he seemed to enjoy throwing campaign buttons to a crowd in New England. At one stop, just as he began to say a few words from the rear platform, a little man in the crowd waved his arms and yelled, "Hello, Woody!" Wilson paused, open-mouthed; then he smiled and waved back. Nobody had ever called him "Woody" before. "At last I feel I have arrived in politics," he told a newsman.

Unlike Bryan and Douglas, Wilson did not limit himself to one issue. He discussed all sorts of public business: tariffs; public

works; labor; conservation; immigration; agriculture. For the
first time a presidential candidate took the people into his confidence, revealed his thoughts, beliefs, intentions. Wilson spoke
the language of broad policies, not specific laws. At New York
he called for "an immense program of social and economic reform
which ought to be undertaken right away;" on tariffs, he argued
that to lower them was to increase American prosperity by encouraging competition; at Boston he said, "I am in favor of the government's building roads and opening waterways and deepening
waterways . . ." He came out strongly for the right to organize,
saying, "I want to widen the market for American labor. I want
to see conditions exist in which men will compete for American
labor. I want men to come to a time again when they will realize
that the highest priced labor in the world is the cheapest labor in the
world."

Among Wilson's favorite themes was the sacred covenant of the
party platform. "If the Democratic party breaks its promises to
the rank and file of the people of this country," he said at the
Armour Packing House, "I hope it will never be trusted again.
Because parties are not merely to put men in office . . . parties are
meant to do the services which they pretend to do when they put
forward their platforms. Their platforms ought to be sacred en-
gagements." Wilson's New Jersey record proved he meant what he
said.

Although the Wilsonian "New Freedom" meant the government
should break up monopolies, Wilson should not be mistaken for a
modern "big government" liberal. His views on individual freedom were as conservative as Barry Goldwater's or the late Robert
Taft's. Too much government, Wilson said repeatedly, is dangerous. "Liberty is its own reward," he said. "I had a thousand
times rather be free than be taken care of." Unlike Goldwater,
however, he wasn't thinking of old-age pensioners and unmarried
mothers on relief. "How long is it going to take businessmen in
America to find out that they have got brains enough not to depend

upon the Ways and Means Committee of the House and the Finance Committees of the Senate," he asked, "not to go to their dear grandmother in Washington and ask her not to let anybody hurt them?" That was the point of the "New Freedom"— freedom to compete by skill and ingenuity in a free market, without benefit of high tariffs or tax loopholes.

In October Wilson's train puffed into Lincoln, Nebraska, Bryan's home town, where he was greeted by nine brass bands, twelve marching clubs, thousands of Democrats, and a great bear hug from The Commoner. (Bryan, to his credit, gave as unstintingly for Wilson as he had for himself, speaking 10 times a day for seven weeks. Wilson later made him Secretary of State.) On October 13, hoarse and worn out, the candidate came home to Princeton. Two days later he received word ex-President Roosevelt had been shot in the chest by a maniac while speaking at Milwaukee. Fortunately the wound was not serious, and TR, brave cowboy that he was, refused medical aid until he finished his speech. Both Wilson and Taft sent regrets and used Roosevelt's convalescence as an excuse to suspend campaigning. For Wilson it meant a much-needed rest.

The professor wound up at Madison Square Garden in late October. He was met by "a wild, waving, cheering, yelling, roaring, stamping mob of enthusiasts that needed no songs and no hymns and no encouragement to keep it at high pitch," said the New York *Herald*. His long tours completed, Wilson made the customary prediction of victory at the polls. And no one doubted he would win.

"There was less political buncombe, less appeal to ancient party slogans, and far more vital discussion of the issues of the time," wrote Ray Stannard Baker, the journalist and Wilson's good friend, of the campaign. "He had no long background of political attachments and obligations, he had made no promises to anyone; he was interested above all in ideas, and in making clear actual conditions as he saw them."

Where Bryan preached an endless sermon of panacea in free silver, Wilson expressed faith in industry, ingenuity, enterprise and freedom—provided each man helped. Woodrow Wilson, in 1912, put the progressive dreams for America into a nationwide mural. He did not make detailed campaign promises; one reads his speeches in vain for the catalogue of pledges John F. Kennedy would splash on the canvas a half century later. Wilson talked principles, not programs. The laws, the policies, he said, would come later—as indeed they did. But in his imaginative discourse, his wish to get across ideas rather than score debater's points, in his candid admission he didn't know every answer, [4] he raised the level of campaign oratory. Wilson, the spiritual ancestor of Franklin Roosevelt, Adlai Stevenson and John Kennedy, made stumping respectable.

As he enlarged the candidate's role, so he also extended the President's. He managed to do this despite having polled only 42 per cent of the popular vote—fewer votes, in fact, than Bryan in any of his three campaigns. Roosevelt and Taft got 50 per cent between them; even Eugene Debs, the Socialist candidate, whose popularity was a good barometer of the reform climate, polled nearly a million votes. Some people wondered whether John Kennedy, who won by a hair more than 50 per cent of the popular vote in 1960, had a "clear mandate" to press his programs. Woodrow Wilson, a real minority President, rejected the notion. In his first term he pushed through Congress a spectacular list of important bills.

Out of Wilson's pledges grew the Underwood Tariff Act of 1913, which cut tariffs; the Clayton Anti-Trust Act to regulate monopolies; the Federal Trade Commission Act aimed at unfair business practices; the Federal Reserve Act to reorganize the nation's credit system; the Farm Loan Act to help agriculture; the La-Follette Seaman's Act to promote safety on shipboard; the Valua-

---

4. "I have no pill against an earthquake," he said. "I have no remedy, but I do know that the things that we have found out that are wrong can be stopped . . ."

tion Act to assist the Interstate Commerce Commission in setting railroad rates. Wilson pressured Congress into repealing the exemption of American ships from Panama Canal tolls, justifying his refusal to support this plank in his platform. The eight-hour-day, workman's compensation laws, anti-child labor laws—all came to fruition in the years of Woodrow Wilson.

This is not to say every law was a model of unyielding idealism. The Clayton Act turned out to be a seriously compromised version of Brandeis' original plan—the definition of a trust was only one flaw. Nor did Wilson ever support such progressive ideas as woman suffrage; when the ladies came to the White House for his help, he ducked behind the Democratic platform, saying the party had no plank on the issue. Still his record of promise and performance stands among the best in American history.

Wilson restored the Democrats to power for the first time since Cleveland in 1892. He did not give the party a clear majority in the country, and Republicans would soon get another chance. Running again in 1916, Wilson used McKinley's front porch technique, speaking from his summer home in Sea Girt, New Jersey, once a week. Even this was a radical departure for incumbent Presidents. McKinley, in his second race, had refused to campaign at all.

Wilson ran on his reform record, but more pointedly on the theme that with Europe in flames since 1914, he had steered the United States clear of "foreign entanglements." Across the country color posters on fences, walls and billboards proclaimed, "He Kept Us Out of War." The President was too honest to believe a slogan he feared, correctly, would soon go sour. Still, he let the voters think he held the magic key. One could not quarrel with peace. Wilson's opponent, the solemn Supreme Court Justice Charles Evans Hughes (whom TR called "Wilson with whiskers"), proposed no dramatic program in opposition to the Democrats. "The human interest of this campaign," wrote Walter Lippmann of Hughes, "is to find out why a man of rare courage and frankness should be wandering around the country trailing nothing but cold and damp platitudes."

Yet the election was close. Wilson got 277 electoral votes to Hughes 254, 9.1 million popular votes to 8.5 [5] It was a personal victory for the President, and his heart was heavy when, five months later, he asked Congress in an eloquent speech to declare war on Germany. Americans sang "Over There," and entered jubilantly into a conflict they were certain would "make the world safe for democracy." The war raised the curtain on Wilson's tragic last act. International fame would be his when the Allies triumphed; but squabbling at the peace table, which he tried and failed to mediate, left him sick and worn out. In Paris he suffered a thrombosis; but no one, not even his doctor, knew it. Back home the GOP stewed because he had refused to take a bi-partisan peace mission to Europe. At the end, Wilson, the political scientist, educator, and stubborn idealist, could not find the means in politics and diplomacy to bring the United States into a League of Nations that would outlaw war from the world.

In 1919 the President made a long whistle-stop tour of America, trying, as in 1912, to educate the citizenry to peace, world co-operation, and America's entry, without reservations, into the League. His efforts failed. The country had lost patience with idealism. In Colorado Wilson's health broke and, partially paralyzed, he returned to the White House, where he finished his term of office in seclusion, remote from his cabinet, the Congress, and the public business. Meanwhile, Republicans in Congress, led by the vindictive Senator Henry Cabot Lodge, defeated America's entry into the League of Nations. Lodge demanded reservations he judged, rightly, Wilson would never accept. Looking backward Wilson's refusal seems petty; it has been suggested his thrombosis

---

5. For more than a day Republicans thought they had won. A reporter, calling on Hughes the day after election, was told, "The President is sleeping." "Well," said the reporter, who had the latest returns, "when he wakes up, tell him he isn't President any more."

impaired his judgment; broken in health and spirit Woodrow Wilson died in 1924.

Wilson foundered on the rock of stubborn pride in 1919. But from 1912 he left a sheaf of mature political speeches that remained an inspiration to the future. He proved a candidate could travel, speak often, shake hands, make headlines, and still retain dignity enough for a President. George Washington would have approved. Moreover, he added vision to technique, and idealism to vision. That's why Wilson's name still crops up in the speeches of Democratic candidates for President, while nobody in the GOP has mentioned McKinley or Taft for 40 years.

Part Three

SITTING ON THE FRONT PORCH

Chapter 6

REPUBLICAN REVOLUTIONARY:

WILLIAM McKINLEY

"The advantages of the front-porch method are overwhelming. The candidate preserves not only his dignity, but also his physical well-being. His speeches, instead of being hurriedly improvised, are prepared with deliberation; they are not echoes of something repeated a dozen times in the past; they have coherence and point, being in each case confined to a single issue. The newspapers, provided with advance copies, print the full text."—Professor Edward McC. Sait, in *American Parties and Elections*, 1942.

Despite the advantages Professor Sait saw in sitting on the front porch in the 1920's, America's last front porch campaign took place years before he wrote. Presidents William McKinley (1897-1901) and Warren Harding (1921-23) between them did nearly all the front porch campaigning that ever was done. [1] McKinley and Harding had many things in common. Both were Republican Presidents from Ohio. Both had served in Congress, McKinley in the House and Harding in the Senate. Each was tall, open faced, handsome, fluent in speech. Both died in office. An assassin shot down McKinley just after he had won a second term in 1900. Harding died mysteriously in California, probably from a blood clot in the brain.

On the ladder of presidential prestige McKinley ranks somewhere near the middle; sympathetic biographies, like Margaret Leech's excellent *In The Days of McKinley*, have increased his stature in recent years. Although Harding deserves pity for his poor taste in friends, there is not much to be done for his stature.

---

1. Benjamin Harrison in 1888 and Wilson in 1916 each made a few front porch speeches; but neither operated on the scale of McKinley and Harding. There have been no other front porch campaigns to speak of.

Only death saved him from impeachment. Historians rate him, with General Grant, a failure. McKinley's accession to office was the point at which the progressive revolution began to affect the national government. Harding's wrote its epitaph. To study McKinley on the front porch is to discover the first faint stirrings of alarm in the GOP over the results of Democratic activity on the stump. To study Harding is to see the mindless imitation of a winning formula by a man certain of nothing— no fact, no issue, no ideal—except that the people would elect him.

Until McKinley no Republican had made any public effort to elect himself President, Harding and Hoover campaigned lackadaisically during the flush 1920's and Coolidge not at all. For "Republican" and prosperity" were synonymous until 1929 in the years when the GOP had no national trauma to live down. It was easy for the party's candidates to adhere to the old tradition of the non-campaign. In those years, any nominee could have worn successfully the protective coloration of economic boom.

Republican candidates moved to the porch not as an alternative to the stump but in transition to it. The front porch campaign was the GOP's way of placing one toe in the swirling waters of the modern campaign. Having got its feet wet, there was no turning back. From the porch to the stump turned out to be a short hop, Herbert Hoover made it with ease though not without misgivings.

William McKinley, born at Niles, Ohio, served in the Union Army while still in his teens. He was the last Civil War veteran to be President. Practicing law in Ohio he turned to politics, won a seat in Congress, and made himself an expert on tariff matters. He attracted the attention of an Ohio industrialist, Marcus Alonzo Hanna, barrel-chested man with bright brown eyes, courage, and a built-in desire to be a king-maker. [2] Hanna picked McKinley as a

------

2. To this day Hanna remains in schoolbooks and memory a gross caricature. The cartoonists of 1896 drew him as a pudgy, evil-faced man, covered with dollar signs, manipulating a puppet labelled "McKinley." In fact McKinley was no man's pup-

likely crown prince and in 1891 helped him become governor of Ohio.

McKinley looked strong, dignified, secure, and sound, with his big but not fleshy face, forthright eyes, aristocratic brow. He spoke well and earnestly, not as a crusader but as one knowledgeable in public affairs. In 1892 Hanna nearly swung the Republican nomination for his man. When it went instead to Benjamin Harrison, Hanna did not fret. He was confident 1896 would be McKinley's year. (So was McKinley. A Boston lawyer named Samuel Powers had the eerie experience of hearing from McKinley's lips the prediction of his own nomination and election in 1892—four years before it happened.) To keep McKinley in the public eye, Hanna sent him stumping across the country, Maine to Minnesota, for Harrison that fall. He made nearly 400 speeches in 300 towns. Senator Jonathan P. Dolliver called him "the advance agent of prosperity."

Four years later, at St. Louis, Hanna put together the nomination for his candidate despite hostility from Eastern Republicans, unhappy with McKinley's pro-silver record; for the Republicans, like the Democrats, had their Western silver faction too, men who were just as fervent for free coinage as Bryan. Led by the peppery Senator Teller of Colorado, the silver men fought for a favorable platform against tough odds. McKinley's straddle, in fact, was to suggest a platform calling for support of "our present standard." He thought, perhaps, if gold were not mentioned by name the silverites could swallow it.

McKinley did not reckon with the fears of the Eastern gold bugs. Their fight to put one word into the platform makes a good case study in the importance of platform writing to party harmony. They insisted the plank should state "the existing *gold* standard

pet; he was a better politician than Hanna and could tell his manager off when he felt it necessary. As for Hanna, William Allen White, who knew him, wrote in the 1940's, "Mark Hanna was an honest, just, ever generous man who had no frills, no side, no nonsense about him, a man with a sense of humor and a sense of loyalty; and I have not changed that opinion in nearly fifty years."

should be preserved." Nothing less would do. McKinley and Hanna, high tariff men, but not very gold conscious, appeared to accede to this plank under great pressure. They still hoped to placate their silver friends from the West.

Hanna, in fact, deliberately left the wording in doubt after it had been settled. The night before the platform was to be read to the convention a small bearded man walked into Hanna's room at the Southern Hotel. "Mr. Hanna," he said, "I insist on a positive declaration for a gold standard plank in the platform."

"Who in hell are you?" asked Hanna.

"Senator Henry Cabot Lodge, of Massachusetts."

"Well, Senator Henry Cabot Lodge of Massachusetts," said Hanna with the greatest contempt, "you can go plumb to hell. You have nothing to say about it." According to the Chicago publisher H. H. Kohlsaat, who reported the incident, Lodge replied, "All right, sir; I will make my fight on the floor of the convention."

Lodge, of course, had no fight to make. The plank he wanted had already been written; later, in fact, he would try to take credit for writing it himself. The final plank also committed the party to oppose the free coinage of silver "except by international agreement with the leading commercial nations of the earth, which agreement we pledge ourselves to promote." This later phrase was inserted at McKinley's insistence to soothe the ruffled feathers of the silver delegates from out West. Senator Teller could not be appeased. Tears running down his cheeks, he made a poignant farewell speech to the GOP he had helped found 40 years earlier and walked out of the convention leading 24 delegates, while those remaining, including Mark Hanna, shouted "Go! Go!"

The platform thus resolved, the Republicans could not ignore Bryan, who had crucified the gold forces in his own party with his "cross of gold" speech. On the money issue the battle had been joined—at least in the party platforms. McKinley's traditional idea of a presidential campaign called for him to operate discreetly from the study of his home in Canton. But Bryan, on a stump procession in the direction of Madison Square Gadren, was attracting great crowds. McKinley faced a dilemma. As Herbert Croly put it, the governor "cherished a high respect for the proprieties of political life and refused to consider a competing tour of his own." After all, this was not the way Republicans did things. Yet Bryan was making a lot of noise and creating favorable attention. When McKinley adamantly refused to commit the indignity of going to the people, Hanna, always practical, decided to bring the people to him.

From June until November McKinley held court on his front porch in Canton, Ohio, every day but Sunday. At first he thought he would simply accommodate those who showed up. He said he was "adverse to anything like an effort being made to bring crowds here." This did not deter Hanna. East and West he recruited visitors for the pilgrimage to Canton. Many delegations were financed by the Republican national committee; others got favorable excursion rates from the railroads, whose loyalty to the GOP was never to be doubted.

Ladies auxiliaries, Union and Confederate veterans, steel workers, farmers, hardware dealers—they flowed into town like lemmings to the sea. As many as 20,000 to 30,000 people descended in a single day, bearing McKinley badges, buttons, caps, capes, canes, umbrellas and horns. They came in costume; they brought their own marching bands; they came in a deluge, making every day circus day with their exuberant parades to the candidate's modest frame house. Once there, they trampled the front lawn brown, and it became a mud puddle in the late summer rains. They wrecked the picket fence and grape arbor, and left the porch rails weakened. Here was democracy in action, the Presidency personified in the people come to seek the man. It found him, statesmanlike, sitting on the front porch with his old mother in a rocker by his side.

Relaxed and smiling, McKinley, wearing a long double-breasted coat, red carnation in his pocket, and white vest, listened, spoke, and presided with unfailing good nature over the destruction of his property. To a casual observer it was all enthusiasm and spontaniety. McKinley was never at loss for exactly the right words. The applause never faltered. But none of the drama was haphazard or improvised. Delegations did not just pop in, unannounced, to demand a speech or grill the candidate. For the likeable, decent, unaffected McKinley was a shrewd and experienced manager of political crowds. His front porch appearances were as well-planned and directed as the movies of Cecil B. DeMille.

Each delegation was asked to have its chairman meet McKinley in advance. The chairman's speech, if he had one, was checked, edited, and, if necessary, revised by McKinley himself.[3] Then the candidate, assisted by his political secretary, Joseph P. Smith, wrote out "remarks" based on the chairman's speech and what they knew to be the visitors' dominant interest. McKinley later replied with taste, spontaneity, and simple dignity to the eager folks on the lawn. His speeches made excellent newspaper copy, too.

During one advance briefing the GOP candidate asked the visiting chairman to read his speech aloud. "My friend," he said, "That is a splendid speech, a magnificent speech. No one could have prepared a better one . . . but is it quite suitable to this particular occasion? Sound and sober as it is . . . I must consider the effect from the party's stand point." McKinley suggested the man go home and rewrite the address along lines he was quick to outline. "Such a method was not calculated to produce bursts of personal eloquence on the part of the chairman," commented Herbert Croly, "but the candidate preferred himself to provide the eloquence."

This McKinley ably did. As one observer said, the Republican nominee "could talk generalities more impressively than any man in public life." Moreover, McKinley had a much better grasp of

---

3. If the chairman had no speech, he was advised to write one and submit it for approval. McKinley was glad to suggest suitable topics.

economics than his opponent Bryan; and he could be quite specific when he chose. McKinley's favorite issue was not gold, anyway, but tariffs. He had always expected to make his campaign on behalf of high tariffs. For the tariff amounted to a tax foreign countries paid for the privilege of selling goods in the United States. Keep tariffs high, and the volume of imported goods remains low. McKinley had sponsored high tariff bills in Congress as a way to protect American business from foreign competition. In his early campaign speeches, the GOP candidate ignored gold and stuck with tariffs. Protection, he insisted, meant high wages, full employment, and business growth. But he also noted tariffs should remain flexible enough to give favorable concessions to countries that wished not only to sell to us but to buy our goods, too.

If McKinley had had his way he would have talked tariffs for four months straight. But Bryan's "16 to 1" silver tour across the country made the Republican gold bugs nervous. They had their platform complete with the word "gold," but they would not sleep soundly until McKinley inserted it into his speeches. Six weeks after his nomination the candidate obliged. "That which we call money, my fellow citizens," he said at last to the McKinley and Hobart Club, of Knoxville, Pennsylvania,[4] "and with which values are measured and settlements made, must be as true as the bushel which measures the grain of the farmer, and as honest as the hours of labor which the man who toils is required to give. Our currency is good—all of it as good as gold—and it is the unfaltering determination of the Republican party to so keep and maintain it forever." The magic word had slipped out, but, commented *The Nation*, McKinley uttered it "in a somewhat furtive way . . . hastening to take a good pull at the tariff to steady his nerves."

McKinley won the biggest popular vote since Grant. The tariff bill, his major campaign promise, passed in 1897, though in a much mangled way. Even this issue began to strike McKinley

---

4. Garret A. Hobart, of New Jersey, was McKinley's 1896 running-mate.

as out of date; he realized American industry had begun to make much more than the nation could use, and he understood, perhaps as well as any man of his time, that the United States would never become a leader in world trade by selling without offering to buy.

Soon McKinley's tariff and Bryan's free silver issues would both be eclipsed by the Spanish-American War. It is this event with which McKinley's name is linked most often today. American sentiment for Cuban independence from Spain had been growing for years, mixed up, no doubt, with a desire by some Americans to acquire new territory for the United States. Before his first term ended, McKinley had asked Congress to make war on Spain, a war which would deliver Puerto Rico and the Philippines into American hands.

So McKinley's most memorable act did not follow from anything that had been discussed in his campaign against Bryan. The people had not elected him to make war on Spain; the issue was not covered by any campaign promise.[5]

Running against Bryan once more in 1900, McKinley refused to go even as far as the front porch. "There will not be visiting delegates or anything like that," he told a journalist. "Four years ago I was a private citizen and the candidate of my party for President. It was my privilege to aid in bringing success to my party by making a campaign. Now I am President of the whole people, and while I am a candidate again, I feel that the proprieties demand that the President should refrain from making a political canvass in his own behalf."

McKinley had reasserted the tradition of aloofness. His attitude could have been built at least partly on self-confidence. Times were good; the Spanish-American war had resulted in a smashing American victory. The Republican party platform had

---

5. In fact relatively few of the really momentous presidential decisions in American history had ever been thrashed out beforehand in an election campaign. Most occur in response to events that were not foreseen during the race.

come out for reform ideas like monoply regulation, "an effective system of labor insurance," and new child labor laws. The "full dinner pail" made a potent slogan.

So the burden of stump speaking was carried in 1900 by the vice-presidential candidate, New York's fiery ex-governor Theodore Roosevelt. Roosevelt was one of the few orators of the day who could match Bryan's skill as a crowd-pleaser; and the tradition of aloofness did not apply to Vice Presidents. Years later Roosevelt said of Bryan, "Well, I drowned him out in 1900. I talked two words to his one. Maybe he was an oratorical cocktail, but I was his chaser."

Mark Hanna stumped for McKinley too, speaking, like Bryan from the rear platform of a train in the West. In South Dakota however, Hanna was forced to change his tactics. The Populist South Dakota legislature had passed a law against politicians addressing political rallies from campaign trains or within 200 feet of the tracks. Populists could not afford the luxury of special trains. This was their way of evening the odds with the richer Republicans and Democrats. So Hanna had a carriage meet his train at each stop in South Dakota. He would be driven a legal distance away, mount a platform and speak, then, at the sound of the whistle, return to his train for a trip to the next stop.

There is no telling what would have happened to the GOP if McKinley had lived out his second term and Roosevelt had succeeded him for eight years. It is possible the Republicans would have made a smooth transition into the 20th century, setting up new party traditions, taking over Bryan's reforms wholesale, and perhaps precluding the Democratic recovery under Wilson. The stagnant years of Harding, Coolidge, and Hoover might never have been. Might-have-beens, however, make poor history. The GOP had nothing to be ashamed of in McKinley; though Roosevelt scared his party's more conservative members, he, too, could have spared them eclipse by agreeing to run in 1908 instead of turning over the job to Taft.

Because of his early death, McKinley's legacy to his party was the protective tariff, a victorious and profitable war, and the front porch. In a rapidly changing world, he did not leave much to build on, and so Warren Harding, when his turn came, stood pat.

Chapter 7

"NOT NOSTRUMS BUT NORMALCY":

WARREN GAMLIEL HARDING

"... not heroism but healing, not nostrums but normalcy,[1]
not revolution but restoration, not agitation but adjustment,
not surgery but serenity, not the dramatic but the dispassion-
ate, not experiment but equipoise, not submergence in inter-
nationality but sustainment in triumphant nationality."
—Senator Warren G. Harding, to the Boston Home Market
Club, May 14, 1920.

One hot summer afternoon in 1919, the story goes, Senator
Boies Penrose, boss of Pennsylvania, called in his colleague Warren Harding, of Ohio. "Harding," he said, "how would you like
to be President?" The second senator's mouth opened, but no
words came. "Why Penrose," he stammered at last, "I haven't
any money and I have my own troubles in Ohio. In fact, I'll be
mighty glad if I can go back to the Senate."

"You don't need any money," Penrose told him. "I'll look
after that. You'll make the McKinley type of candidate. You
look the part. You can make a front porch campaign like Mc-
Kinley's and we'll do the rest."

Harding's nomination was still a year away. At the GOP convention of 1920 the front-runners were General Leonard Wood,
Army hero, and Governor Frank Lowden, of Illinois. For nine
ballots these two deadlocked the convention. Party leaders buzz-
ed in and out of the suite of editor George Harvey, of *Harvey's*

---

1. Harding used the word "normalcy" in a speech ghostwritten for him by Professor
Jacob H. Hollander, of Johns Hopkins University. Years later the professor told
Eric Goldman he had written the word "normality" but Harding mis-read it. "Poor
Warren Harding," said Hollander. "What he did with that word showed a lot that
was wrong with the man."

Weekly, on the top floor of Chicago's Blackstone Hotel. This was the famous "smokefilled room" wherein, according to the prediction of Harding's floor manager Harry Daugherty, "at about eleven minutes after two, Friday morning of the convention, when ten or twenty weary men are sitting around a table, someone will say, 'Who will we nominate?' At that decisive time the friends of Harding will suggest him and can well afford to abide by the result."

By one contempory account, Boies Penrose, sick and in a coma at Philadelphia, roused for a minute and asked his secretary Leighton Taylor, how the convention was going. Taylor said it was deadlocked. "Call up King and tell him to throw it to Harding," said Penrose, nudging the fates in the direction of his own prophecy.

Harding made an ideal compromise candidate. He looked good —over six feet tall, dark hair and even teeth, a fine mouth. He had a clear voice that carried well, and fancied himself an orator for his abstract, cushiony speeches. In a year that demanded compromise, Harding was its essence. He had been on all sides of every important public issue, notably the League of Nations, prohibition and women's rights. Over the League, Republicans suffered a thousand agonies. Many of them—Charles Evans Hughes, ex-president Taft, Elihu Root for example—wanted in. Old progressives, the anti-war isolationists like Senator Hiram Johnson of California, and Senator William Borah of Idaho, wanted no part of more "entangling alliances" in Europe. To make these two wings flap in harmony fell to Warren Harding.

"This year we had a lot of second raters," said Senator Frank Brandegee, of Connecticut. "Harding is no world-beater. But he's the best of the second raters." [2] Yet, in his bumbling, dense, amiable way he proved perfectly equal to the task of being the 1920

---

2. Samuel Hopkins Adams, who reported this statement, said that Harding might have been a second-rate senator, but "As a potential President, he was a tenth rater."

Republican candidate. His success guaranteed the Republican party 12 unbroken years of build-up to the biggest let-down in American history.

Harding was born in Corsica, Ohio, November 2, 1865. He went to Ohio Central College, acquired a newspaper, the Marion *Star*, and settled down to a life on Main Street. He dabbled in politics, married an ambitious woman five years his senior (he called her "Duchess"), went to the state senate, became Ohio's lieutenant governor in 1904-5, but lost a race for governor in 1910. Popular, easy-to-get-along-with, a good drinking companion, susceptible to instruction, Harding made an ideal machine candidate for Senate in 1915. He served as temporary chairman of the Republican convention in 1916, and attracted favorable notice with his fine voice.[3]

By 1920 Harding was well known to the party; there was little to be said against him. "Harding stands for the kind of candid and unpretentious reaction that anyone can respect, and that a great many people momentarily desire," commented *The New Republic*. Who can blame Republicans if the tractable Ohio senator reminded them of another Ohioan, the revered William McKinley, of blessed memory?

So they moved McKinley's old flagpole from Canton to Harding's front lawn in Marion. There Warren Harding began one of the strangest and most confusing campaigns on record. He liked the front porch. He wore a carnation (like McKinley), played horseshoes out back with visiting politicians, and thrust his large, muscular paw at every caller. He loved to shake hands. "It's the most pleasant thing I do," he once confessed in a statement hardly to be doubted. And the front porch, said Harding, speaking with the voice of Republican tradition, protected the dignity of

---

3. He was not so happy with his speech, though. "It's rotten," he told Finley Peter Dunne, in a revealing statement. "I wrote a good one, but my friends in the Senate made me put things in—the tariff, reciprocity, public lands, pensions, and God knows what—and now it's a rag carpet."

a would-be President. What's more, it "assured correct public version of deliberate statements."

Meanwhile, the Democrats had trouble finding a candidate. Wilson, an invalid in the White House, sick and bitter over Congress' rejection of his plan for the League, insisted on a pro-League platform and a pro-League nominee to stand on it. Yet the party politicians knew America had grown tired of the League, of war, of Europe, of the endless conferences. Long gone were the days when the school children of Paris threw flowers at Wilson's feet and his countrymen considered him the greatest man in the world.

Wilson in 1920, meant political hot water for the Democrats. German-Americans, for example, blamed him for not keeping the country out of war in 1917. Irish-Americans blamed him for not supporting Irish independence at the Paris peace table. Italian-Americans felt let down at his failure to back Italy's plan to annex Fiume. Though Wilson's son-in-law William Gibbs McAdoo, wanted the nomination, his family ties made him an unlikely candidate. Bryan, still active, tried to steer the party his way with a strong prohibition plank and a compromise plan for the League of Nations. Nobody would listen to him; for the first time in memory he would sit out a campaign. After 44 ballots the weary delegates lit on James M. Cox, three-time reform governor of Ohio, a man almost unheard of outside his home state, but with no ties to Wilson either.

Cox, a stubby, bespectacled, serious-minded dynamo, had made himself a millionaire in newspaper publishing. He had strong labor sympathies, was a skilled campaigner, and made up in political shrewdness what he lacked in color and warmth. He chose a genial young New Yorker, Franklin Roosevelt, who had made a good record as assistant secretary of the Navy under Wilson, and had a magic name,[4] as his running-mate. Against the advice of the

---

4. "If he is Theodore Roosevelt," said the Chicago *Tribune*, "then Elihu Root is Gene Debs, and Bryan is a brewer."

party dopesters Cox and Roosevelt went to see Wilson in the
White House. The sight of the President sitting in a wheel chair,
a shawl covering his useless left arm, brought tears to Cox's eyes.
"Mr. President," he said "we are going to be a million per cent
with you and your Administration, and that means the League of
Nations." Wilson raised his eyes. "I'm very grateful," he said.
"I'm very grateful."

Under the tug of emotion Cox sat down in the Executive Offices
and wrote out a pro-League statement for reporters. In it, he set
irrevocably the course he would steer in the campaign. The act
took courage and conscience; Cox lacked neither, but in 1920 the
impulse to avoid being wrapped in the same package of distrust
with Wilson might have been excused in any politician.[5] "Cox will
be defeated not by those who dislike him but by those who dislike
Wilson," predicted the Democratic Secretary of the Interior,
Franklin K. Lane.

In Wall Street the smart money was laying 7 to 1 on Harding. Cox didn't kid himself about the odds. Like every Democrat in this century handicapped by lack of votes he decided to go
on the stump. His campaign, he said, would be "the most stren-
uous ever undertaken by a nominee for the Presidency." He would
skip only the states of the Old Confederacy, those so deeply rooted
in the Democratic party it would take a political earthquake to
budge them. Between September 2 and October 3 Cox visited
every state west of the Mississippi except Arkansas, Louisiana and
Texas. Returning to Ohio, he swung east and blanketed the Mid-
dle-Atlantic, New England, and border states. In two months
he traveled more miles than Bryan (22,000), and delivered 394
scheduled speeches in 36 states. Although he did not speak as
often as the Commoner had, Cox did give 26 speeches in one ex-
hausting day; he was hoarse, nervous and worn out at the finish.

---

5. His courage certainly cost him votes; but there is no reason to believe that had
he been less courageous he would have won the elcetion.

Meanwhile, back on the porch, Harding was practicing one of the neatest circus stunts in the history of politics. He was attempting to balance on one foot upon Elihu Root's League of Nations platform plank and face two ways simultaneously. The plank called for "agreement among the nations to preserve the peace of the world," but "without surrendering the right of the American people to exercise its judgment and its power in favor of justice and peace." Pro-League senators like Root himself believed the first part meant the United States would eventually join the world organization. Anti-League senators like Borah preferred to interpret the last part to mean the country would join nothing it could not control.

Assisted by editor Harvey, Harding sent up his first League trial balloon in late August. He had voted for the League with reservations in the Senate, he said, "most reluctantly and with grave misgivings." Cox was in favor of joining Wilson's League. "I am not," said Harding. Instead, he preferred a "judcial tribunal to be governed by fixed and definable principles of law," like the Hague Tribunal,[6] rather than an "association of diplomats and politicians," which presumably meant the League of Nations. Harding preferred to "combine all that is good and exorcise all that is bad in both organizations." That was Harding in high gear.

The pro-League senators winced at this absurd ambiguity, but the anti-League men got downright jumpy. Was Harding edging toward the League? Senator Borah returned his travel money to the national committee and said he had decided to suspend campaigning. For a month more Harding talked, on the front porch, about some sort of "association" of nations. His comments were like a mirror in which each man might see reflected his own biases. The Boston *Post* was convinced if Harding won, the United States

---

6. The Hague Tribunal, or Permanent Court of Arbitration, had been set up by international agreement in 1899. It could arbitrate only those cases all parties would agree to submit, and so was not kept terribly busy.

would never enter the League. The Republican New York *Tribune*, on the other hand, was confident his statements left room for entry with reservations.

Cox, meantime, was drawing good crowds and, if not wild enthusiasm, a respectful hearing for his ideas. "I am for the League," he said, but added he might accept some self-imposed restrictions on America's entry. As reports of Cox's speeches filtered back to Marion, the Harding managers became edgy. Support from the Borah-Johnson group seemed to have fallen with the autumn leaves; in October it was decided Harding too should take the stump. Before the campaign ended he would speak in the Midwest, some border states, New York, Pennsylvania, and Maryland. In Des Moines, October 7, Harding raised a new balloon. Of the League Covenant he said, "I do not want to clarify these obligations; I want to turn my back on them. It is not interpretation, but rejection, that I am seeking . . . The issue, herefore, is clear . . . In simple words it is that he [Cox] favors going into the Paris League and I favor staying out."

With this speech Republicans played musical chairs again. The word "rejection" had done it. Staunch pro-League party members, like the banker Thomas W. Lamont, bolted the party. The presidents of Oberlin, Vassar, Smith, Bryn Mawr and Mount Holyoke were among 121 Republican defectors who signed a statement urging the election of Cox. On the other hand, "rejection" turned out to be the key to Senator Borah's heart; the old progressive returned to the stump in Harding's behalf. When Cox accused his opponent of "wobbling," Harding offered a reward to anyone who could prove "any inconsistency or change" in his position. Nobody could, since it would require pinning down his position to begin with.

So Harding stood with one foot on his platform, one eye on the conservatives, and the other foot in his mouth. On the porch, on the stump, he indulged his fine voice in the most meaningless abstractions ever uttered by a would-be President. Once, reading a

speech ghosted for him either by Harvey or the fiction writer
Richard Washburn Child, Harding stopped, stumbled, started
over, then looked up and smiled. "Well, I never saw this before,"
he admitted. "I didn't write this speech and I don't believe what I
just read."

He had charm. Nobody could get very mad at Harding. Each
Republican faction, knowing their candidate to be flexible, felt
sure he *really* leaned toward it.[7] Finally, to bail Harding out of the
sea of ambiguities buffeting the Republican ship, the party's intellectual leaders—any one of them would have made a better
nominee—drafted a "Declaration of Thirty-One Proleague Republicans." It said flatly the GOP would take the United States
into the League; the only problem to be resolved was which reservations to attach. Herbert Hoover, Henry Stimson, Elihu Root,
William Allen White, and Charles Evans Hughes, among
others, signed the statement. Their plan—to draw up a world
court proposal and submit it to the League—mollified the isolationists. Deep down Borah and Johnson were convinced Harding
belonged to them.

Harding did not discuss only the League issue. He said, for
example, he favored collective bargaining by labor and management; he accepted a Republican plank (forced in by the progressives) covering employment of women and children. He agreed
there should be a federal department of public welfare and government aid to housing. His pledges sounded vague but sincere.
Who could doubt he meant it when he said, at Buffalo, he wanted
"an America to continue where childhood had a right to happiness,
motherhood to health, everyone to education, and all Americans
the right to our equal opportunity . . . an example of a government
always responsive, always understanding, always humane."

Harding's resemblance to McKinley ceased when he opened his

---

7. Richard Nixon and Thomas Dewey are other candidates of recent memory who
could throw diverse Republicans into a similar hypnotic trance.

mouth. Like his spiritual ancestor on the porch, he stood for high tariffs; but he could not really say why. "More business in government and less government in business," summed up Harding's economics. He promised, if elected, to reduce the income tax. He denounced excess profits taxes as unfair (to consumers!).

By election day nobody—except perhaps Wilson, isolated in the White House—believed Harding could be beaten. The only question remained how big his victory would be. Its size astonished even the experts. Warren G. Harding, received 404 electoral votes from 37 states to Cox's 127. Only the South voted Democratic, and not so solidly—Tennesee, Oklahoma, and West Virginia went for Harding. He received a whopping 16.1 million votes to 9.1 for Cox. The little town, largely German, of Bismarck, North Dakota, which had gone 100 to 2 for Wilson in 1916, exactly reversed itself in the rush to elect Harding. So the worst President in history won the most overwhelming victory ever given a presidential candidate in the United States to his time.

In the White House Harding served drinks to his poker buddies, carried on an affair with his mistress, and lamented privately he couldn't understand the public business that came to his desk. He ducked and sidestepped the League issue as fumblingly after election as before; nothing came of it. In his first message to Congress he ignored various welfare proposals the liberal Republicans had put in the platform. Instead, he spoke up for federal aid to maternity hospitals and nurses—an issue so far out in left field the platform writers had specifically rejected it! Congress spent most of its time on tariffs, a subject hardly mentioned during the campaign. That was okay with Harding. He was willing to leave Congress alone; kindly, good-natured, ignorant, he allowed himself to be swayed like a palm in every wind.

Meantime, the "Ohio Gang," including Attorney General Daugherty, were buying and selling favors on a scale beyond belief. Secretary of the Interior Albert B. Fall was running his own little

market in government oil leases. Harding mercifully died before
the scandals were fully revealed, and it fell to President Coolidge to
clean up the mess.[8]

William Allen White judged the country had got what it bargained for in Harding. The United States, he wrote, "after eight
years of Wilson and the four short years of breathing space with
Taft before Wilson, and seven years of Roosevelt—almost 20 years
in which people were keyed up to principles, years in which causes
were followed and battles fought for issues rather than men—was
tired of issues, sick at heart of ideals and weary of being noble."

That summed up Harding's success on the porch and Cox's
failure on the stump. For 12 years more no Republican would
need to make a serious campaign to win the Presidency. Times
got richer. The Republicans remained solidly entrenched during
the 1920's. For the average voter it was hard to see how far the
party of McKinley and Roosevelt had slid down the long hill of
reaction to become the party of Harding, Coolidge and Hoover.
While the world moved, the Republicans sat on the front porch.
Only the Democrats stumped seriously in the Golden '20's, trying
to get the electorate's ear. For the Democrats were bursting with
internal pressures; soon the seams would split, and a dramatic
realignment of American voters would alter the nature of campaigns for good.

---

8. It took years. Fall was not convicted of anything until 1929, when he was found
guilty of accepting a bribe. The government could never make stick the charge of
conspiring to defraud the nation.

Part Four

THE MODERN CAMPAIGN

Chapter 8

LET'S LOOK AT THE RECORD:

ALFRED EMANUEL SMITH

"Somewhere on the sidewalks of New York, without benefit of the moral training on tap in Kansas and Mississippi,
he picked up the doctrine that it is better, after all, to be
honest than to lie. It is not a popular doctrine in America.
It is a dangerous baggage in politics. It gets a man suspected and hated . . ."—H. L. Mencken, August 27, 1928

June 1924. Madison Square Garden. William Jennings Bryan,
64, hair gray and thin, paced up and down restlessly. They had
drawn a "speaker's corral" in chalk on the platform, like a batter's
box; but the aging orator kept straying and had to be reminded
continually to talk into the mike. For the first time in history a
national convention was being broadcast; it mattered little that
Bryan could still work up enough steam to project the great voice
of 1896 through the heat and smoke and tepid air of the Garden.

What they listened to was the longest, bitterest intra-party feud
since the Douglas fiasco of 1860. "My friends," Bryan was saying, "it takes more courage to fight the Republican party than the
Ku Klux Klan." From the galleries came boos and catcalls. The
moment symbolized the eve of a major revolution in the Democratic
party; the power balance was shifting away from the dry, rural,
Anglo-Saxon Protestant constituency Bryan had built in the West
and South. Now the Boy Orator who had transfixed the Democrats with gold crosses at Chicago 28 years earlier, stood, an old
man, muttering an inane defense of the cross-burning Klan within shouting distance of Tammany Hall.

For Tammany's votes came from Italian, Irish, Polish, Slavic
and German immigrants, and their children, many of Catholic or
Jewish descent. Their hero was Governor Alfred E. Smith, of New

93

York, a gusty Catholic Irishman from the Manhattan streets, outspoken foe of prohibition, bitter enemy of the Klan. Al Smith
came to the convention of 1924 with nearly a third of the delegates
in his pocket.[1] New York governors had always been serious
presidential contenders; Bryan, backed by friends in the West and
South, had his own candidate, Wilson's son-in-law, the ever-avail-
able William Gibbs McAdoo, of California.

Now Bryan asked the delegates not to condemn the Ku Klux
Klan by name; the Klan, a post-Civil War throwback, had risen
again in the wake of World War I. Dressed in robes and hoods,
its members went around setting crosses on fire to dramatize their
antipathy toward Catholics, Jews, Negroes, and all "foreigners"
and "outsiders." Bryan, sweating and tired, sought to protect the
pro-Klan delegates for his man McAdoo, a staunch prohibtionist,
who also had supported a vague platform plank to "condemn any
effort to arouse racial or religous dissension." Northern Democrats
around Al Smith insisted the Klan be named. The issue came to
vote; and Bryan, who would die within a year, succeeded, by 4
votes, in keeping the platform vague.

But they booed him from the galleries. The common people of
New York City in 1924 had nothing in common with the Great
Commoner from Lincoln, Nebraska; yet it was they who would
soon add to the party the vitality it needed to win elections. The
convention dragged on day after day—McAdoo vs. Smith—ballot
after ballot. By mid-July the delegates had taken 70 ballots
without a decision—13 more than the record-breaking convention
of 1860 which tried, and failed, to nominate Douglas. On July 21
Smith and McAdoo both gave up. John W. Davis, a lawyer who
had been a congressman, solicitor general, and ambassador to
England, became the Democratic nominee. Davis was one of the
best qualified men ever nominated to be President; yet at the

---

1. Those who saw the movie "Sunrise at Campobello" may recall the final scene
when Franklin Roosevelt walks forward on crutches to the cheers of the crowd. He
was rising to nominate Al Smith in the convention of 1924.

moment of his victory, on the 103rd ballot, no bookmaker would give decent odds he could win. The voters out in radioland had had more than enough of the Democratic family feud.

Bryan, the city-bred Al Smith, the Klan, and the Democrats hung up for two weeks to pick, at last, a West Virginia intellectual who made it his first order of business to denounce the Klan too:[2] these were the ingredients of a symbolic changing of the guard; for the West and South had tried to block Al Smith's candidacy, but, as the Newark *News* put it, "Governor Smith emerges from the Democratic wreck a bigger figure than ever before." John Davis waged a dignified, energetic campaign from coast to coast in 1924, a model for underdog Democrats. Calvin Coolidge kept cool in the White House, ignored Davis, uttered hardly a word, and won handily. Many potential Davis votes were pulled off by the flamboyant Robert LaFollette, of Wisconsin, a renegade Republican, who tried and failed to revive the Progressive party of old.

Could the Democratic party survive its clash of regions, religions, and preferences in drink? It seemed plain unless the hatchet could be buried in 1928 the party might break up for good. A politician summed up the Democratic trauma of 1928 in a letter to McAdoo. Smith, he wrote, made his appeal "to the aliens, who felt that the older America, the America of Anglo-Saxon stock, is a hateful thing which must be overturned and humiliated." These were the Negroes, Catholics and Jews. "If the dominance of such groups represents the new America which Smith is seeking to arouse, the Old America of Jackson, and of Lincoln and Wilson, should rise up in wrath to defeat it." Perhaps McAdoo recognized that the "new" America would one day open the door to victory for the "old." He withdrew his candidacy to save the party.

In this he showed good judgment, for the new immigrants, far

---

2. Davis pledged a liberal program in line with his undoubted sympathies; but three years in a Wall Street law firm had made him anathema to liberal Democrats. To placate Bryan the convention picked his brother, Charles W., former governor of Nebraska, to run with Davis; and thousands voted against the ticket, mistaking Charles for William Jennings making a fourth try.

from wanting to humiliate old America, wanted more than anything else to succeed in it—and by the old standards. Al Smith
was moved by a desire to show that a poor boy from the New
York sidewalks could grow up to be presidential timber. For a
century the average President had been born and raised in upstate
New York or a small town in Ohio. He was a businessman, lawyer, country editor, or soldier. He belonged, practicing or not,
to a respectable Protestant sect; his ancestors (like everybody's)
had been immigrants, too, but they came long ago from Northern
Europe or the British Isles and were called "pioneers" instead.

These were the traits of the men who governed the United States
at least from the time of Andrew Jackson. After the Civil War,
newer immigrants—Catholics and Jews from Central, Eastern and
Southern Europe—sailed to America and settled in the coast cities.
The newcomers struggled to feed and educate their children; and
the children—for whom Al Smith became a beacon—started the
long climb up the ladder of public life. Governor Smith of New
York represented not a threat to America, but proof of its capacity
to grow.

Smith's log cabin had been a lower East Side tenement, where
he was born when General Grant was still President. Altar boy,
newsboy, factory hand, graduate of the Fulton Fish Market, he
joined the New York Democratic Organization, which was called
Tammany Hall, before he was 21.[3] He learned politics from the
precincts up, becoming in turn member of the State Assembly,
sheriff of New York County, a member of the New York City
Board of Aldermen. Between 1918 and 1928 he won the governorship of New York state four times—a record—and gave the
state, among other things, a capital budget, welfare reforms, a new
executive structure, and the best administration it had ever had.

With his ruddy, open face, sharp blue eyes, compact athletic

---

3. Once the subject of college degrees came up on the floor of the New York State
Assembly. Smith rose to explain he too had a degree: FFM. Asked what that was,
he said, "Fulton Fish Market."

build, and inevitable derby hat, he made a popular and attractive politician. He spoke in a raucous East side accent ("foist" for "first"), but those who heard him had to agree he knew what he was talking about. He had an instinctive sympathy for the people he served. He was much more "the commoner" than Bryan; moreover, he was not a panacea-peddler, but a man curious to understand the intricacies of public business and communicate them to others. Smith, said one aide, "could make statistics sit up and beg, roll over and bark."

The Democratic Convention of 1928, meeting in Houston, with McAdoo out of the picture, could hardly deny Al Smith its highest honor. Wet, Catholic, and of Tammany Hall, he might be. He was also the best candidate available. The South and West had no hero to rally round; Al Smith was nominated in one ballot.

To avoid prohibition, the year's thorniest issue, the party climbed up on the fence. For nearly a decade it had been illegal to make, sell or drink alcoholic beverages in the United States. Yet, from the day of its passage, prohibition had been flouted openly and badly enforced. Anybody who wanted to could make gin in the bathtub and many did. But the drys maintained one of the all-time great lobbies in American history. When they turned on the heat every politician perspired, especially in the South and Mid-West. So the Democratic platform of 1928 pledged "the party and its nominees to an honest effort to enforce the 18th Amendment and all other provisions of the federal Constitution and all laws enacted pursuant thereto." This did not mean all Democrats opposed drinking; it meant they stood four-square behind the Volstead Act, which opposed drinking.

Smith, whose weakness was candor bordering on lack of tact, kicked this plank out of his campaign. "It only dodges and ducks," he told friends in Albany, and sent a wire to the Houston convention outlining his real stand. "If you send that telegram you may not be nominated," he was told. "I'd just as soon not be nominated as to stand for something I don't believe in," he replied. The telegram went forth calling for "fundamental changes in the present provisions for national prohibition." It arrived as the Convention was adjourning. Democratic drys, feeling they had just done the governor a big favor by nominating him, considered the message an ungrateful kick in the teeth from that Tammany Catholic. Many of them would abstain from campaigning; a few would vote Republican—and hate Al Smith for having made them do it.

Meanwhile the Republicans, at Kansas City, had put up Herbert C. Hoover, Secretary of Commerce, whose chief, President Coolidge, had said he did "not choose to run." Hoover came equipped with a classic American background of humble beginnings, hard work, spectacular success. He left his Iowa birthplace as a boy to live with California relatives, graduated from Stanford University as a mining engineer, speculated in mine enterprises around the world. By age 40 he was a millionaire. Hoover knew how to get a job done. During World War I he earned an international reputation distributing food and clothing in France and Belgium. Later he became United States food administrator; his name became a household word: to "hooverize" meant to save food.

Hoover tugged at Republican and Democratic imaginations as the moon upon the tides. Like Eisenhower years later, both parties wanted him for a candidate. After the war he concluded he was a Republican and accepted a spot in Harding's cabinet. Aloofness was Hoover's middle name. An engineer by profession, an administrator by temperament, he had no more use for politicians than the Anti-Saloon League for rum. He was among the few Harding cabinet members unblemished by the scandals of the 1920's. The GOP had no trouble nominating the most distinguished non-political figure of the period as proof of the party's basic integrity.

Beneath his smooth, moon-like face Hoover wore a high collar popular 15 years before. Sober, thrifty, capable, of Quaker ancestry, "he smokes grimly," reported one observer. He did not drink at all. His prose, in contrast to Smith's, was heavy, plodding, full of platitudes. It seemed, said Richard Hofstadter, like "a light fog moving over a bleak landscape."

The Republican nominee's acceptance speech laid down the barrage of prosperity propaganda behind which he moved doggedly toward the White House. "We in America are nearer the final triumph over poverty than ever before in the history of any land," he said. He cited 9 million homes with electricity, 6 million telephones, 7 million radios, 14 million automobiles, and countless parks, playgrounds, and roads—all created by American ingenuity, hard work, and—with a bow toward Harding and Coolidge—"the wisdom of our national policies." Should the Republicans be "given a chance to go forward with the policies of the last eight years, we shall soon, with the help of God, be in sight of the day when poverty will be banished from this nation."

As a candidate, Hoover shunned campaigning. He made rare "dignified" appearances talking generalities on tariffs, farm prices, and government economy. He spoke no more than half a dozen times, never mentioned Smith by name, and did not argue a single issue. The heavy work was left to sloganeers:

HOOVER AND HAPPINESS OR SMITH AND SOUP HOUSES?
WHICH SHALL IT BE?

The only serious issue, said Hoover, was prosperity. The GOP had delivered. The Democrats could not. Yet the GOP's power base had grown narrower since 1900. Samuel Gompers and the labor movement had gone over to the Democrats nearly 20 years before. As the internal conflicts between Smith and Bryan proved, the Democratic party was spreading out. Power was shifting east again, but not into the hands of the descendents of Grover Cleveland's gold cabal. In politics he is strongest who has the votes, and Al Smith had become what is known as "a proven vote-getter."

Smith's strength gave him a claim upon the Presidency; but his religion left him vulnerable to attack. In 1927 a New York lawyer, Charles Marshall, published an "open letter" to Smith in the pages of the *Atlantic Monthly*. It was temperate, literate, and well informed, but the gist was this: How could a Catholic President, considering various Papal encyclicals serve his church and his country both?

In reply Smith cited his New York state record back to 1902. "I have taken the oath of office in this state 19 times," he wrote. "Each time I swore to defend and maintain the Constitution of the United States . . .I have never known any conflict between my official duties and my religious beliefs." He closed with "a fervent prayer that never again in this land will any public servant be challenged because of the faith in which he has tried to walk humbly with his God."

His prayer proved futile. Pamphlets, leaflets, letters, and cartoons from underground presses, blanketed the country. A typical anti-Catholic flyer showed Governor Smith at the opening of the new Holland Tunnel which joined Manhattan and New Jersey under the Hudson River. If elected, said the caption, Smith would extend the tunnel beneath the Atlantic Ocean to the Vatican's basement, an engineering feat no more remarkable than the 3000-plus-miles pilgrimage the Pope would then make—underground—to take over the United States.

One scholar turned up the fact that in 1928, the 152nd year of American independence, many people believed the Constitution prohibited Catholic Presidents. Still others acknowledged an "unwritten law" to the same effect. "Mr. Hoover, himself, and the National Committee," wrote a GOP committeewoman in Virginia, "are depending on the women to save our country . . . from being Romanized and rum-ridden." Though Hoover quickly repudiated this letter which "did violence to every instinct I possess," most of the time he simply ignored the religious issue.

Smith was called "rum-soaked Romanist" in the South by otherwise good Democrats, who, militantly dry, considered drinking vile sin. It's hard to tell where religion ended in 1928 and whiskey began, so mixed up were the two issues in the psyches of millions of people. For many drys, Smith's religion was significant only because it did not forbid liquor. '

Al Smith, who had built his New York career upon candor, had no qualms about saying prohibitionists, like the king, had no clothes. He called the Volstead Act a farce that bred disrespect for laws, corrupted revenue agents, and created a new industry called bootlegging. Smith's specific proposal was modest enough. Let Congress define what it meant by "alcoholic beverage," and raise the legal limit on alcoholic content. Then let each state legislate drinking to suit itself.

Hoover avoided this issue as he did most others. His platform called for enforcement of the Volstead Act. In February he wrote the dry-as-dust Senator Borah that prohibition was "a great social and economic experiment, noble in motive and far-reaching in purpose." This wholesome viewpoint suited the ladies of the Women's Christian Temperance Union, who did not believe a God-fearing man might want to decide for himself what he would drink. Methodist Bishop James Cannon, Jr., a lifelong Democrat, aroused the South on behalf of Hoover and against Smith, ostensibly over liquor.[5] But, as Virginius Dabney wrote, Cannon also "hauled in the religious issue, and he emphasized it, played upon it, and reiterated it until this political campaign throughout the southern states was transformed into what was tantamount to a religious war." (Cannon also spread the rumor the East Wing of the White House would be the Pope's American home.)

The jaunty, self-assured Smith, meanwhile, was making plans to take the sidewalks of New York to Main Street. Of all the

4. Despite Will Rogers' comment that Mississippi would vote dry as long as the voters could stagger to the polls, there appear to have been some people anti-liquor but not anti-Catholic—including even a few Cathoilcs.

5. The best that can be said for Hoover and liquor was that he was dryer than Smith, and much quieter. Senator Carter Glass, Democrat of Virginia, offered $1,000 if anyone would come up with a single categorical "dry" statement by Herbert Hoover. He had no takers.

Democratic stumpers stretching back 68 years to Stephen Douglas none came better equipped. He was no spellbinder like Bryan, but as Walter Lippmann commented, "He was able to fascinate great audiences with the business of financing and administrating public affairs and to make them share his own interest in problems that the ordinary public relations expert would say were too dull and over people's heads."

Lacking Wilson's theoretical powers, Smith made up this deficiency with hard study: he was interested in how, not why. It seemed obvious to him every citizen should have a decent house, enough to eat, and the right to decide for himself what he would drink. Furthermore, he believed government had a stake in these matters, and, as a descendent of Wilson, he had a passion to educate people to his beliefs. He could be utterly convincing. "His mastery of the subject was his real stock in trade," said Lippmann. "No one who heard him had the least doubt that he knew what he was talking about."

The Smith campaign train, equipped for the first time with three radio receivers (including one for reporters in the club car) sped across the nation. Despite the undercurrent of religious hostility, it was met everywhere by great crowds. Their enthusiasm seemed real enough, as Smith, brown derby on his head, unlit cigar clamped in his teeth, tried to throw the issues into the void of Hoover's vast silence. Wagging his head briskly from side to side, he deftly punctured the Hoover prosperity balloon. His favorite gambit was to read and comment on Republican campaign literature. At Boston he took for his text the flyer headed A CHICKEN IN EVERY POT.

" 'Republican prosperity has reduced hours and increased earning capacity,' " quoted Smith. "And then it goes on to say Republican prosperity has put a chicken in every pot and a car in every backyard to boot."

He shook his head in disbelief. "I wonder what idea the man who invented a thing like that had in his mind? What must be his estimation of the average intelligence of the Amreican people?

"Here's another good one for you," he continued. " 'Republican efficiency has filled the workingman's dinner pail and his gasoline tank besides, and placed the whole nation in the silk stocking class, and made the telephone, radio, and sanitary plumbing standard household equipment.'

"Now just draw on your imagination for a moment, and see if you can in your mind's eye picture a man working at $17.50 a week going out to a chicken dinner in his own automobile with silk socks on."

The speech illustrated Smith's special talent: he would quickly relate an abstraction like "prosperity" to one man in the audience —the factory worker who earned $17.50 a week. Yet Smith's frankness—his almost obsessive wish to speak his mind clearly and accurately on every issue—did not always work to his advantage. Liberals loved him for it, but many potential Smith voters were scared off.

Take immigration. A National Origins Quota Act had cut off the great wave of immigration in the early 1920's. Smith backed the Democratic platform which supported existing laws "in full force and effect," except where families might be broken up. His views differed hardly at all from Hoover's; but Hoover saw no point in stirring up the melting pot. "Mr. Smith, the candidate of Tammany," charged a Republican bulletin, "by his own statement, believes in lifting restrictions on certain classes of aliens. His idea is that of the typical New Yorker and not that of the rest of the country." In the Carolinas they advised Smith to avoid two subjects: immigration and tariffs. Stubborn and hardheaded, he spoke on nothing else.

At Louisville he encountered a patronage police force which had recently gone Republican when the city administration changed hands. The cops were obviously hostile, and were suspected of turning up the steam heat when the hall where Smith spoke grew unbearably hot. As he left, a policeman passed the word to

reporters that Smith was drunk.° When the Louisville *Courier*
denounced the local police some residents wrote Smith asking him
to correct the "erroneous" impression of their city. He couldn't,
he replied. It was all true.

Peeling away issues, one always reached the underground
stream of anti-Catholicism. This matter, Smith believed, could
never be dealt with by ignoring it. Characteristically, he felt it
should be dragged out of the closet, exposed, and got rid of at the
outset. That's how conflicts were settled on the New York streets;
the process worked in state government; people respected a man
who didn't hem and haw. Proud of his humble origins, Smith felt
sure people in the Mid-West and South would respond to simple
appeals to reason, fairness, and justice.

He decided religion should be the theme of his second major
speech, at Oklahoma City. Oklahoma in the 1920's raised not only
cattle and wheat in abundance but Ku Klux Klansmen. His advisers told Smith to leave religion alone. No, said the candidate,
sooner or later the issue must be faced, and it might as well be in
the enemy's country. "I felt deep in my heart," he recalled, "that
I would be a coward and probably unfit to be President if I were
to permit it to go further unchallenged."

Oklahoma City greeted Smith with tremendous crowds; but his
friends, fearing violence, borrowed soldiers' uniforms and dressed
up a group of volunteers as a body guard. At the Oklahoma Coli-
seum, 10,000 seats quickly filled and thousands of people crowded
the hallways and waited outside. When Smith rose to speak they
cheered for a full minute. Religion, he said at once, was a word
that "should never be used in a political campaign." But he
owned it to the voters to discuss the subject openly, this attempt
"to inject bigotry, hatred, intolerance" into what should be an "in-
telligent debate of the important issues."

For an hour, to a noisy audience frequently shouting approval,

---

6. The rumor that Smith was always drunk and had to be held up by two men
wherever he went was spread across the country.

he reeled off facts and figures, and named names. People hooted when he mentioned the Grand Dragon of the Klan of Arkansas. He denounced the WCTU, and Mrs. Mabel Walker Willebrandt, a United States assistant attorney general for prohibition enforcement, who made partisan anti-Smith speeches to church groups.

One by one he took up and refuted the whispered lies. Did he, for example, appoint only Catholics and Jews in New York State? His cabinet contained 10 Protestants, 3 Catholics, 1 Jew. Building to a climax, he attacked the Ku Klux Klan again. "The world knows no greater mockery than the use of the blazing cross, the cross upon which Christ died, as a symbol to instill into the hearts of men a hatred of their brethren, while Christ preached and died for the love and brotherhood of man."

The Oklahomans cheered, clapped and stamped their feet, a commotion some radio listeners took to be protest. Back in Albany Smith's family feared he would be attacked. Later he told them the main noise came from a man sitting half way back yelling, "Pour it on 'em Al, pour it on 'em!"

Al Smith's Oklahoma City speech ranks among the great presidential campaign documents. He composed it—as he did all his speeches—on his feet, from a few notes scribbled on envelopes he had picked up here and there. But it stated in a clear and dramatic way what it meant to America to have an Irish Catholic from the Lower East Side running for the office first dignified by George Washington. Smith made no pretensions to aloofness. This was a luxury Democrats could not afford. But he put a much more substantive matter up for public consideration, the proposition that America either gave every citizen the same chance, or the Founders' ideals were a mockery.

There have always been citizens unwilling to accept the proposition; but in 1928 they were much more outspoken than today. The Reverend Mordecai Fowler Ham, for example, who had sat in the audience at Oklahoma City, later told his flock, "If you vote for Al Smith, you're voting against Christ and you'll all be damned." As the Smith campaign train steamed west, a cross could be seen burning against the sky at Rim Rock near Billings, Montana.

Al Smith also mastered the use of the radio and the microphone —the gadget that had baffled Bryan. Radio became an important instrument of politics in 1928 for the first time. As governor of New York Smith had figured out he could make a speech every night for 30 nights straight and only talk to 30,000 people—about one per cent of the electorate. On the radio he could reach millions with a single address.[7]

Major J. Andrew White, president of CBS, compared the radio personalities of the candidates for the New York *Times*. "Hoover is cold in his radio delivery," he wrote. "He speaks as he would to an audience in a hall." Smith churning out facts, anecdotes, and wit "is as interesting and gripping at the fireside or on the front porch as . . . in a hall with thousands present. Radio transmits his magnetic personality whereas it even further chills Hoover's delivery of cold facts."

Yet Al Smith, in the Democratic tradition, also went straight to the people, as Douglas, Bryan, and Wilson had done. Hoover, walking the path of Harding and Coolidge, confident of his party's dominance, held aloof. Nevertheless, he won by 444 electoral votes to 87, 21.3 million popular votes to 16 million. It was a humiliating defeat for the Happy Warrior. Aside from Massachusetts and Rhode Island, Smith captured only six states of the deep South. His own New York, where he had been the most popular governor in history, preferred Hoover for President—although the ticket-splitters crossed over and elected Democrat Franklin Roosevelt as Smith's successor. Herbert Hoover became the first Republican to win Democratic states like Texas, Florida, North

---

7. Al Smith also was the first presidential candidate to appear on television. His acceptance speech at Albany, August 22, 1928 was picked up and broadcast by General Electric to its Schenectady plant 15 miles away by a "strange, box-like contraption with a lens on front."

Carolina, Kentucky, and Tennessee. He had broken the solid South wide open.

Many people still believe Al Smith lost the election of 1928 because he was a Catholic and Herbert Hoover wasn't. The test of this belief is whether Smith might have won had he not been Catholic, and the answer—as long as we leave him his Tammany background and wet sentiments—seems to be "no." In 1928 prosperity conquered all. Hoover can be excused for claiming Republicans caused the rising stock market of 1928. He "said what he correctly judged the majority of voters thought, and promised what the majority wanted," observed Elmer Davis. "Adult Americans elected him for the same reason that would have led Americans under the age of 10 to elect Santa Claus."

Al Smith was not only the Catholic candidate, he was also the wet candidate; and a lot of God-fearing people saw the election as a national referendum on drinking. Professor William F. Ogburn, studying 173 Northern counties, decided that "prohibition sentiment was three times more decisive an influence . . . than the religious issue." His analysis seems reinforced by the boast of the drys they won 48 of 53 governorships (including territories), and most of the state legislatures. (Their victory, of course, was like the last brilliant flash of a meteorite before it burns itself out. Repeal was only four years away.)

More important than the way Hoover won, however, is the way Smith lost. Roosevelt would soon repair the cracks in the solid South. But the GOP had yielded for the indefinite future the big city vote. Al Smith—wet, Irish-Catholic, Tammany Democrat, antithesis of the dry, Anglo-Saxon, Protestant, rural Bryan—succeeded at last where Bryan had failed. He brought millions of voters in the urban areas of the East and Mid-West into the Democratic party. Since 1860 the "party of rebellion" had been a moon in partial eclipse. Only the South was dependably Democratic. In 1928 although the North went Republican, cities like New York, Boston, St. Louis, San Francisco, Cleveland, and Milwaukee swung to Al Smith. Upon the party of the KKK in the South, Smith permanently affixed the balance wheel of urban minority groups in the North. He created the coalition Franklin Roosevelt would use to restore to robust health the party that had almost commited suicide listening to the aging Bryan in 1924. Bryan, had he lived, would not have enjoyed the irony.

The greatest irony of 1928, however, was that Santa Claus never came. Hoover made one unbeatable campaign promise: continuing prosperity. He could never deliver on it. He was unable to avoid the stock market crash of 1929. He could not prevent the dust bowl that wiped out so many farmers in 1930. Like a character in Greek tragedy, the able, efficient Hoover watched from the White House while the temple of America affluence crashed all around him.

The Great Depression was the GOP's Civil War. It wiped the party off the map of politics for 20 years. Since 1896 the Republicans had made economic progress the party's claim upon the American voter's loyalty; when progress collapsed, so did the party. The election of 1928 ended the GOP's adherence to the tradition of aloofness. From 1932 onward, Republican candidates, too, would stump, whistle-stop, and in general imitate the behavior once considered reprehensible—in Democrats. But the party would find it hard to recover the confidence of voters in its ability to keep the economy booming. To this day the GOP still gropes toward an alternative to Franklin Roosevelt's New Deal.

Chapter 9

THE DEMOCRATIC RENAISSANCE:

FRANKLIN DELANO ROOSEVELT

"Welcome to Roosevelt From the Forgotten Man"—Sign
carried by a group of shabbily-dressed men in Los Angeles,
1932 campaign.

Consider first the man. He was born at Hyde Park, New York, January 30, 1882. Six months earlier James A. Garfield had been shot by an assassin; Chester A. Arthur was President.[1] When Bryan fireballed across the East in behalf of free silver and the Common Man, Franklin D. Roosevelt had just enrolled at Groton, the most exclusive boy's school in America. He graduated from Harvard in 1904, married a distant cousin, (another cousin, President Theodore Roosevelt, came to the wedding), attended Columbia law school, and in 1910 entered politics as a state senator from Dutchess County. In 1912 he yelled for Woodrow Wilson at the Baltimore Convention and was re-elected to the state senate. His manager was a tough, disheveled little reporter named Louis Howe.

From 1913 to 1920 he served as assistant secretary of the Navy under Wilson. Tall, debonair, with a winning smile, sometimes a bit pretentious, Roosevelt made friends easily in Washington. His famous name was thought to make him a good running-mate for James Cox in 1920. Traveling the country by train, he spoke nearly 1000 times; he and Louis Howe took mental notes on the art of campaigning; his smile and strong walk became a familiar sight.

---

1. When he was 7 his father, a staunch Democrat, took him to the White House to see President Cleveland. "My little man," said Cleveland, patting his head, "I am making a strange wish for you. It is that you may never be President of the United States."

In August of 1921, sailing with his family at Campobello Island near New Brunswick, he spotted a forest fire on shore. He and the children beat out the fire with evergreen branches, trotted through the woods, swam in the icy Bay of Fundy, then ran home in wet bathing suits. Next morning, trying to get out of bed, he felt pains in his legs. "I don't know what is the matter with me, Louis," he told Howe. "I just don't know." Both legs were paralyzed. Doctors soon diagnosed the trouble as polio. They said he would never walk again.

Now consider the country. During the 1920's, while Roosevelt struggled to regain his legs, the United States had taken a holiday. Liquor was illegal, but everybody knew President Harding kept an open stock on the second floor of the White House to serve his poker friends. The stock market had gone up, up, up, first under Coolidge, then under Hoover, who promised two cars in every garage in 1928. In this climate it was not hard to forget the disillusioning last years of Wilson and the failure of the League of Nations. Said John J. Raskob, Democratic national chairman (a Horatio Alger character who had gone from $7.50 a week stenographer to chairman of the finance committee of General Motors), "I am firm in my belief that anyone not only can be rich, but ought to be rich." The year was 1929.

In October the American economy, staggering under the weight of speculators with other peoples' money, began a dizzy roller coaster ride over the peak of prosperity. "There has been a little distress selling on the Stock Exchange," said Thomas Lamont, of J. P. Morgan and Co., as an incredible 13 million shares changed hands in one day. United States Steel, selling for $261 a share September 3, was worth only $150 November 13. Nobody seemed to know where the other $111 had gone.

The roller coaster sped downhill. By 1930, 6 million people had no jobs, by 1931, 10 million, by 1932, 15 million. A $45 a week stenographer in 1929, if she was still working, now made

$16. Her husband, out of work, waited in a bread line. Most states had no unemployment compensation, or public assistance. Social security was unknown. When a man lost his job he sold apples at 5c each; people soon grew sick of apples. "It can't get any worse," Americans said in 1930; but it did. President Hoover watched helplessly as farm prices melted to nothing, banks and factories closed. He tried what he could. He asked Congress for a public works program to make jobs. He asked for money to loan farmers whose crops were ruined by drought. He set up a Reconstruction Finance Corporation to prop up faltering banks, businesses, railroads. Nothing helped.

Will Rogers neatly summed up the Republican dilemma of 1932: "All the Democrats have to do is promise what they would do if they got in," he said. "But the Republicans have to promise what they would do and then explain why they haven't already done it." The GOP had been glad to take credit for the prosperity of 1928. Could it escape blame for the Depression of 1932? It would try. Herbert Hoover was renominated at Chicago in June on a platform that blamed the Depression on events in Europe over which Republicans had no control. The United States, meanwhile, was as flat on its back as Franklin Roosevelt had been.

"Legs or no legs, Franklin will be President," said Louis Howe. Roosevelt spent a good bit of time in the healing waters of a run-down resort at Warm Springs, Ga. He dramatized his recovery by staggering forward on crutches to nominate Al Smith in the 1924 Democratic convention. Out of the bitter Ku Klux Klan fight that year Roosevelt emerged "the most popular figure in the convention," said Virginia's Harry Byrd. When FDR nominated Smith again in 1928, he used heavy leg braces and a cane. As governor of New York he pushed forward with Smith's reform politics and was re-elected by a land slide in 1930. Two years later he shouldered Al Smith aside. Dealing with the Bryan-McAdoo faction, Roosevelt agreed to accept the lusty Speaker of the House

John Nance Garner, of Texas, as his running-mate, and he was nominated for President in return. [2]

FDR had an intuitive sense of drama. The Depression had been a national trauma, like the Civil War. It called for unprecedented behavior. Roosevelt told reporters he would accept the nomination in person; in fact, he twitted them, he planned to ride to Chicago on a 5-seater bike with his four sons behind him. On the morning of July 2 he took off from Albany airport with his wife, his sons John and Elliott, and Samuel Rosenman, a lawyer and close adviser. The flight to Chicago against strong headwinds took nine hours, with stops for fuel in Buffalo and Cleveland. Around 6 p.m., loking fresh and relaxed in a blue suit, with a red rose in the lapel, FDR appeared on the rostrum. He was the first candidate to accept his nomination at a national convention.

Nearly four months earlier Rosenman had remarked, "If you were to be nominated tomorrow and had to start a campaign trip within ten days we'd be in an awful fix." The New York governor had no program to alleviate the national depression. The customary advisers—businessmen and politicians—had failed to come up with answers for Herbert Hoover. "Why not go to the universities of the country?" asked Rosenman. The professors "wouldn't be afraid to strike out on new paths just because they are new."

As governor of New York FDR had sometimes asked Raymond Moley, of Columbia University's department of government, to draft speeches. Now he called upon Moley to organize a cadre of idea men to formulate a Democratic program. Moley enlisted two colleagues, Rexford G. Tugwell, an economist, for farm problems, and Adolph A. Berle, Jr., of the law school, for credit matters.

---

2. Smith never forgave him. In 1928 the Happy Warrior said he would not seek office again, but like TR in 1912, he changed his mind, and found, too late, that Roosevelt had sewed up the convention. Thereafter Smith opposed FDR at every turn. Unhappily, in this negative role, his immense talents were lost to the nation for the last 15 years of his life.

This was the start of the "brain trust," which was to give Roosevelt a post-graduate course in national problem-solving. Meanwhile, Moley began work on an acceptance speech he was not sure FDR would deliver.

Then, at Chicago, the moment came. "I have started out on the tasks that lie ahead," said Roosevelt, "by breaking the absurd tradition that the candidate should remain in professed ignorance of what has happened for weeks until he is formally notified . . . You have nominated me and I know it, and I am here to thank you for the honor.

"Let it also be symbolic that in so doing I broke tradition. Let it from now on be the task of our Party to break foolish traditions."

Bowing to the memory of the "progressive soul of our Commander-in-Chief, Woodrow Wilson," he endorsed the party's platfrom ("I accept it one hundred per cent.") and pledged that he would "leave no doubt or ambiguity on where I stand on any question of moment in this campaign." [3] (Roosevelt's platform, one of the briefest in years—fewer than 2000 words—succinctly stated what was needed to put the nation back on its feet. It demanded a 25 per cent reduction in federal spending, a balanced budget, public works, unemployment and old age insurance, control of crop surpluses, regulation of utilities and holding companies, protection for bank deposits, repeal of prohibition, and "international agreements for the reduction of armaments." [4]

With charm and self-assurance the first crippled candidate promised to restore the crippled economy: "Millions of our citizens cherish the hope that their old standards of living and of thought have not gone forever. Those millions cannot and shall not hope

---

3. This pledge, worthy of Al Smith's successor, sounded convincing; but on some issues FDR would certainly leave doubt where he stood, for he could not be sure himself.

4. Barry Goldwater said in a TV interview in 1964 he thought he could run on a platform similar to FDR's in 1932, "the most conservative platform of this century." Evidently he stopped reading after the first two planks.

in vain. I pledge you, I pledge myself, to a new deal for the American people. . ."

So the New Deal was born.[5] The details had not been worked out; how the program would be explained to the voters remained inconclusive. Senate Democrats advised Roosevelt against stumping. Wilson was the only candidate to do it and win—but the Republican party had split to give him a three-way race. Stick to the radio, he was told; hold a few ballyhoo rallies in the East. "All you have to do," argued his running-mate Garner, "is stay alive until election day." At Chicago a reporter asked Roosevelt if he planned to campaign in all states. "No, I hardly think so," said FDR. "You know, those coast-to-coast trips are all right for a young man such as I was when I was a candidate for Vice-President and I was only 38." Then he added significantly, "But things are different now." Yet he was not old—only 50. What made things "different" perhaps (he would not say it) was the condition of his legs.

On July 4 he said he would make only six or seven radio speeches—on prohibition, public utlities, farm and tariff matters, unemployment and relief, taxes and government spending, and foreign affairs. Back in Albany he raised the question of stumping with his campaign manager, the genial James A. Farley, a national chairman noted for his elephantine ability to connect faces with names. Democratic congressmen frowned on a stump tour, Farley reminded him. They sugested the front porch. "Jim, what do you think yourself?" asked Roosevelt.

"I think you ought to go and I know you are going anyway," Farley told him.

---

5. There are many versions of the origin of the phrase "New Deal." Raymond Moley says he wrote it in a memo to FDR. According to Arthur Schlesinger, Jr., Samuel Rosenman, editing Moley's draft of the acceptance speech, put in the words, perhaps after reading Stuart Chase's article "A New Deal for America" in that week's *New Republic*. FDR himself claimed to have taken the phrase from Mark Twain's Connecticut Yankee, who said, "when six men out of a thousand crack the whip over their fellows' backs, 'it seemed to me that what the 994 other dupes needed was a new deal'."

"That's right," FDR said slowly "I have a streak of Dutch stubborness in me, and the Dutch is up this time. I'm going campaigning to the Pacific Coast and will discuss every important issue of the campaign in a series of speeches." Behind the decision lay a desire to show the voters by example he was a man who allowed no handicaps to thwart him.

Roosevelt quickly disposed of the prohibition issue, where Hoover was most vulnerable. The President had accepted a plank in the Republican platform pledging to enforce the dry law but adding, "The people should have an opportunity to pass upon a proposed Amendment" which would turn the issue back to the states. In his acceptance Hoover as much as admitted prohibition was a failure.[6] At Chicago Roosevelt left no doubt of his position. "I say to you now," he declared, "that from this date on the Eighteenth Amendment is doomed." A few weeks later he added the Republican platform had been written to sound dry to drys and wet to wets, "but to the consternation of the high priests it sounded dry to the wets and wet to the drys." With the economy tottering, even an astute politician like Roosevelt could not take the Anti-Saloon League seriously; by 1932 the issue that had beat Al Smith was a national joke.

Hoover, meanwhile, immersed in problems at the White House, had come to the odd conclusion Roosevelt would be a lightweight candidate. He announced he would make only three or four dignified speeches. Otherwise, he would stay on the job, fighting the depression from Washington. The Republican National Committee took 40 rooms at the Waldorf in New York for their main campaign headquarters. They set up a western command post in a Chicago hotel. The candidate, they felt, could safely remain aloof, as good Republicans always had done in the days of the

---

6. Hoover could not escape his dilemma. He wanted to hold on to the dry vote if he could. But the Wickersham Commission, which he had appointed to study prohibition and recommend changes in the law, confirmed that the things Al Smith had said in 1928 were all too true.

party's glory. This decision was soon to be reversed. As Bryan
pulled McKinley from the family library to the front porch, as
Cox frightened Harding from the porch to the stump, so FDR's
successful whistle-stopping would push the tired Hoover out of
the White House, most reluctantly, for a stump tour of his own.
He was the first incumbent President to do it, except for Taft,
whose feeble voice had been drowned out by Wilson and Theodore
Roosevelt in 1912.

By mid-September Roosevelt was ready to board his special
train. It had fewer cars than Al Smith's; the Democrats had no
wish to look ostentatious to hard-pinched Western farmers. A
special car for the candidate, a sleeping car and drawing-room
car, lounge and diner made up the train. Roosevelt was joined
by his daughter Anna, son James, Raymond Moley, and a New
England banker named Joseph P. Kennedy, whose 15-year-old
boy John Fitzgerald was struggling that year with Latin at Choate
school in Connecticut. Several dozen reporters and photographers
came too.

Roosevelt announced his first swing would cover 8,000 miles
and 20 states, and would be a "look, listen and learn trip." He
wanted to find out what farmers, in particular, were suffering
that fall. "The Roosevelt managers are convinced that they have a
real chance to sweep many states which usually vote under the
eagle,"[7] reported the *New York Times*, "and they have avowed
that a visit by the candidate himself will materially aid the cause."
Referring to FDR's paralysis, the report continued, "It is hoped
also that the 21-day swing will do much to discount stories that
the governor is not physically able to withstand the rigors of the
Presidency."

Immense crowds greeted Roosevelt everywhere. At Paris, Ill-
nois, where no stop was scheduled, 500 people stood on the tracks
to bring the train to a halt; they would not move until FDR came

---

7. The symbol of an eagle was used on the ballot in many states to identify the
Republican ticket.

out and waved from the rear platform. Next day at Topeka, Kansas, Roosevelt gave a major speech on farm problems. The 1929 prosperity had not done farmers any good, he said. "This nation cannot endure if it is half 'boom' and half 'broke,' " he said in paraphrase of Lincoln. If elected, he would ease farm credit to prevent foreclosed mortgages, readjust tariffs to encourage world trade and get rid of crop surpluses, put pressure on local governments to cut taxes on farmers. "We must have, I assert with all possible emphasis, national planning in agriculture . . ." said Roosevelt. "He also presented a six point program of principles," reported the *New York Times*, "which, while not offering any very concrete plan, formed a basis for something more definite to be worked out after advice from those best fitted to suggest remedies."

In fact no fewer than 25 farm experts, under Moley's supervision, had contributed to the final draft of the farm speech. One of them, M. L. Wilson, an obscure professor at Montana State College, would later become an assistant secretary of agriculture. It was a good example of the brain trust in action—the collective expertise of a large group helping FDR do what previous candidates did alone, or with the aid of a few advisers whose milieu was the backroom rather than the classroom. Roosevelt institutionalized the task force of university experts.

In his first campaign, FDR, expanding on Al Smith's technique of one major issue per speech, covered the broadest spectrum of issues any candidate had ever confronted. At Salt Lake City he proposed another six-point program for railroad regulation under the Interstate Commerce Commission. At Seattle 30,000 people, the largest political crowd in the city's history, turned out to hear him call for" a tariff policy based on reason." At Portland he spoke on public power—the need for "a national yardstick to prevent extortion against the public and to encourage the wider use of that servant of the people—electric power." At the close he added, "I promise you this: Never shall the Federal Government part with its sovereignty or with its control over its power resources, while I am President of the United States." (Out of this promise would grow the imaginative Tennessee Valley Authority.)

By this time the Republicans were growing nervous. Reports from the West all favored Roosevelt. From Washington came an attack on FDR by Joseph M. Dixon, an assistant secretary of the Interior. Dixon, who had managed Teddy Roosevelt's 1912 campaign, proclaimed FDR a cheap imitation of a great President. For example, said Dixon indignantly, the candidate had deliberately imitated TR's pet expression telling the people of Salt Lake City he was "*dee*lighted" to be there. "At Denver and at Butte, in the midst of the old 16 to 1 country," said Dixon, "he assured them of his 'friendliness' for silver and assured them if elected President, he was going to call an international conference. . . ." Nonsense, said Dixon. He had heard "the real Roosevelt at Butte in 1900 . . . lay down in unvarnished words that could not be mistaken the pure and unadulterated doctrine of the *gold* standard." That, critic Dixon implied, took real guts—though he neglected to mention free silver by 1900 was a dead issue.

The next day Roosevelt, at San Francisco's Commonwealth Club, gave one of his finest campaign speeches. The frontier, he said, had been closed. "We are not able to invite the immigration from Europe to share our endless plenty. We are now providing a drab living for our own people . . ." At the rate the country is going, a dozen corporations would control all industry in a hundred years. Businesmen must accept the responsibility that goes with size, and the government's job is to see to it that they do. Whatever the platform said about budget and spending, Roosevelt—in his speeches on railroads, tariffs, public power, utilities, and now business monopoly—left no doubt he stood for an enlarged federal role. The 1929 mess occurred, he implied, for lack of restraint on free enterprise. No one should have the freedom to destroy public confidence in the economy.

Roosevelt's appeal was a calm one, lacking all demagoguery,

though the times were ripe for a demagogue. Ernest K. Lindley, a friendly reporter, said Roosevelt was "no popular idol during the Presidential campaign of 1932." Yet people flocked to see and hear him, or just to wave to him as his train sped past. At countless whistle-stops Roosevelt—like Wilson 20 years before—came out to the rear platform for a hello and a round of handshakes and small talk; he never failed to meet a sympathetic crowd. "The country yearned for a Messiah," Lindley wrote. "Mr. Roosevelt did not look or sound like a Messiah." Instead, he turned out to be a pleasant man, who wore his hat at a jaunty angle, sometimes waved a cigarette holder, nearly always smiled, and joked about leaning on the arm of "my little boy Jimmy" (who was 6' 3"). At countless meetings in hot fields, stuffy auditoriums, or dusty crossroads, a million people saw him clump forward on the heavy leg braces, cane in one hand, to stand firm and confident and tell them the depression could be licked.

Roosevelt's equanimity in the face of his own handicap inspired equanimity. His optimism was contagious. Fewer than 10 years before he had been condemned to bed or a wheelchair for life. Yet there he stood, on a rear platform, at a forgotten rail siding no passenger train had used in years, laughing, joking, and assuring them—as the Democratic candidate for President—that better times lay ahead, that jobs would be restored, that their farms could be salvaged, that their children would be fed. "In all the years of my husband's public life," said Eleanor Roosevelt, "I never once heard him make a remark which indicated that any crisis could not be solved." On the stump, from New York to Kansas to California, Roosevelt's confidence and concern for other people's misery, was communicated in a hundred covert ways.

There was no disease Roosevelt could not treat. He outlined plans for unemployment insurance, old age pensions, mental health clinics, and prison reform. He emphasized local governments should try to find jobs for people, but if they couldn't the state should; if the state couldn't, then "the Federal government should and must provide temporary work wherever that is possible." The nation, he said, "has a positive duty to see that no citizen shall starve." Taken in toto it was a grand performance: in 27 major speeches and several dozen minor ones, Governor Roosevelt, traveling 13,000 miles in 36 states, had outlined the most ambitious plan of government action of any major presidential candidate in history.

Unlike Bryan, Wilson, or Al Smith, he rarely spoke extemporaneously. His speeches were carefully worked out in advance, usually by Moley, with advice from other experts. One associate called Roosevelt "the best picker of brains who ever lived." Not a theoretician like Wilson, lacking Bryan's love of his own words and obsession with panacea, Roosevelt was much closer to Al Smith in his pragmatic approach to problems; but he never employed outright candor if the political situation required subtlety in his judgment. His radio voice was superb; he spoke clearly, with excellent diction. "But above all," said one radio network executive, "it has a tone of perfect sincerity, a quality that we consider supremely essential." When Roosevelt said "My friends," every listener believed him.

It would be misleading to say FDR had every ailment diagnosed right, or that every pill he recommended worked. He could be vague, he could be contradictory. He hated to offend associates, and would more often exasperate (and sometimes alienate) them by failing to tell them outright what was on his mind. Once he flabbergasted Moley by asking him to "weave together" two contradictory tariff proposals that had emanated from the brain trust. And at Pittsburgh he blandly repeated that reduced government spending was a major campaign issue. Hoover had been a spendthrift, commented the man who, as President, would elevate national expenditures to Olympian levels. The Federal budget, he said erroneously, works like a family budget. It was okay to go into debt for a year or to two but not indefinitely. "I shall approach the problem of carrying out the plain precept of our Party, which is to reduce the cost of current Federal Government operation by 25 per cent". Like Hoover's abolition of poverty in 1928, Roosevelt's 25 per cent budget cut in 1932 was pure fantasy; [8] nobody dreamed how much the New Deal would cost.

Yet, being accused of inconsistency, of "veering left and right," didn't seem to annoy Roosevelt. "Let's concentrate upon one thing," he told an associate. "Save the people and the nation and, if we have to change our minds twice every day to accomplish that end, we should do it."

President Hoover, meanwhile, had been stirred out of his uneasy White House aloofness. He had read Roosevelt's Topeka farm speech. He had seen newspaper pictures of the swarming crowds. For three years he had exhausted himself fighting an economic collapse that defied his best efforts. Weary, disdaining politics, he felt now he had to take the stump in defense of his policies. "The only possibility of winning the election, which is lost now," he told Secretary of State Henry Stimson, "would be exciting a fear of what Roosevelt would do."

On this depressing mission the President set out by train, traveling 10,000 miles, delivering five major speeches in October and three in November. The tour brought him no joy. At Des Moines 2000 shabby members of the Farm Holiday movement greeted him with placards reading: IN HOOVER WE TRUSTED: NOW WE ARE BUSTED. It reminded him of the Harding funeral train, he remarked. In contrast to the buoyant Roosevelt, Hoover, bitter at Democratic atacks on his administration, made a gloomy stumper. His appeals were wholly negative as he tried to undercut the ebullient FDR.

He called Roosevelt's promise to put 10 million men to work on

---

8. The 25 per cent cut remains today a part of the glory dream of erstwhile conservatives. Senator Harry Byrd, Democrat of Virginia, the Senate's leading economizer, claimed in 1964 to be the "last of the old New Dealers," for he still favored that 25 per cent reduction and a balanced budget. "Rosevelt changed," said Senator Byrd, "but I did not."

public projects "a promise no government can fulfill." He added,
"It is utterly wrong to delude suffering men and women with such
assurances." Yet the President's contention that the depression
was a result of "world conditions" lent scant comfort to the
sufferers. At Madison Square Garden he slashed at the New Deal
as a "proposal of revolutionary changes which would undermine
and destroy the fundamentals of the American system of government." Roosevelt would not only increase federal spending, he
said, but destroy the government's credit, cut tariff revenues, and
undermine the Supreme Court. "The grass will grow in the streets
of a hundred cities, a thousand towns," he intoned. "The weeds
will overrun the fields of millions of farms" should Roosevelt win.

But Hoover's stock as a social prophet had fallen with the market. FDR won more decisively than Hoover had over Al Smith.
The nation gave New York's crippled governor 472 electoral votes
—more than any candidate in history—against Hoover's 59. He
received 22.8 million popular votes out of 38.5 million cast.
Roosevelt captured 42 of the 48 states including, as his managers
intended, a number of those normally voting "under the eagle."
Not only did he bring back the Southern states that had deserted
Al Smith, he held on to the cities, the working people, the immigrants who had gone Democratic in 1928. And he won more farmers than Bryan—with his free silver panacea—had ever been able
to do.

Roosevelt took Douglas's lost South and charmed its leaders
into living with repeal. The dry cause, south of the Mason-Dixon
line, approached secession in the strength of the feelings it gen-
erated. By making the South swallow repeal, FDR forced the
elixir of life into the region, its politicians, and the Democratic
party. In 1932 he returned the party to a dominant position it
had not enjoyed since before the Civil War.

Roosevelt's first dramatic act after inauguration was to close
the nation's tottering banks. Then began the frantic first 100
days, when an incredible series of bills streamed through Congress

under Roosevelt's firm command. Prohibition was repealed; but even before ratification Congress legalized 3.2 beer, and the experiment "noble in motive" and condemned to failure became not-quite-believable history. An Emergency Banking Act was passed, an Agricultural Adjustment Act to shore up sagging farm prices, a National Industrial Recovery Act to help business, a Home Owners Loan Act, an Emergency Relief Act, and Emergency Railroad Transportation Act. The Civilian Conservation Corps made jobs and helped conserve resources; the Tennessee Valley Authority permanently changed the economy of an entire depressed region. One legislator said the Roosevelt program read "like the book of Genesis." Some of the acts of the first 100 days were later declared unconstitutional by the Supreme Court. Yet, whatever else he did, Roosevelt restored confidence. He offered every citizen a task; he insisted the nation could solve its problems.

Whatever his shortcomings, of temperament, of philosophy, no one could accuse Franklin Roosevelt of lack of initiative or dedication to the task of putting the country back on its feet. "If you had spent two years in bed trying to wiggle your big toe," he once told a friend, "after that anything else would seem easy!"

When Roosevelt forced Hoover out of the White House and into the campaign train, he not only upset the party balance in America; he also reversed the Republican party's conception of how their candidate should run for President. The Democrats had abandoned the tradition of aloofness with Stephen Douglas in 1860. The Republicans remained willing prisoners of the tradition for years afterwards. They stuck to the mystical facade of "dignity" not because they needed it to win, but simply because a natural winner could afford to pretend to be George Washington. A natural loser could not.

Landon, Willkie, and Dewey saw no alternative to the stump in the years Roosevelt, the champion campaigner, towered over the Presidency. They did not imagine the office could be won the

way Lincoln did it, in splendid isolation, or in the McKinley-
Harding manner from a front porch. They went out by train and
by plane and fought hard for Republican restoration. They were
not experts yet—FDR was beneficiary of decades of Democratic
experience—but they tried to copy Roosevelt, on the radio, on the
platform, at the whistlestops. They even tried to copy his promises
—a better break for America; and when they failed, the tattered
remants of the Republican Old Guard would accuse them of being
"me too" candidates who had not offered the voters a useful choice.
In the clinch, Roosevelt's challengers revealed their party's weakness by reverting to the "dire prediction" school of campaign
technique, which had failed Hoover in 1928.

Roosevelt campaigned hard in 1936, the first incumbent President in history to whistle-stop and win. His honeymoon with
Congressional Republicans, businessmen, and bankers ended by
1934. He was attacked unmercifully in the press.[9] He was
slandered and vilified by underground handbills. People whispered he had lost his mind. A *New Yorker* cartoon showed a group
of well-dressed, obviously upper-class, people standing outside a
beautiful home. "Come along," read the caption, "We're going
to the Trans-Lux to hiss Roosevelt."

Among the more respectable attackers was the new American
Liberty League, whose members included Rockefellers, Morgans,
and Duponts. It was also the last refuge of bitter Democrats—
for example, John Raskob, John W. Davis, and Al Smith—who
broke with FDR ostensibly over economic policy. One League
spokesman declared that, "The program choked down the throat of

---

9. "The 1936 election witnessed perhaps the strongest effort in the city's history by
the local businessmen (industrialists and bankers) to stampede local opinion in behalf
of a single presidential candidate," reported Robert and Helen Lynd, in *Middletown in-
Transition*, 1937. The men who controlled the town's jobs and newspapers applied
pressure for Landon. That Roosevelt won so heavily in normally-Republican Middletown the Lynds attribute mainly to the radio. The local power elite could not censor
FDR's compelling speeches over the major networks.

the Congress fulfills to the letter the promises . . . of the Socialist Party." [10]

Roosevelt viewed the campaign of 1936 as a referendum on the success of the New Deal. "There is only one issue in this campaign," he told Moley, "It's myself, and the people must be either for me or against me." To the criticism of big business, Roosevelt replied with the story of the old man in the high silk hat, no swimmer, who fell off a pier one day. "Help, save me!" he shouted. A young man jumped into the water and pulled him to shore; but the silk hat floated out to sea. For years, said FDR with a chuckle, all the old man did was complain about his lost hat.

Roosevelt stumped the Mid-West and East to enormous crowds. At Chicago the streets were lined with cheering people for five miles; 100,000 heard him say, at the Stadium, "It was this Administration which saved the system of private and free enterprise after it had been dragged to the brink of ruin by these same leaders who now try to scare you." Later, at Madison Square Garden, he repeated the remarkable catalogue of Democratic commitments. "Our vision of the future contains more than promises," he said. "Of course we will continue to seek to improve working conditions . . . to reduce hours over-long, to increase wages that spell starvation, to end the labor of children, to wipe out sweatshops." He went on to touch upon the whole list of human problems: public, private, business, labor, farm. It was an astounding performance, not for what he promised, but for the recognition in a single campaign speech that each of these items was the President's business: end monopoly; stop unfair competition; supply cheaper electrcity; aid transportation; reduce interest rates; wipe out slums; cut crop surpluses; control floods and droughts; provide useful work; aid the blind, aged, sick; keep consumer

---

10. This was somewhat short of the truth. The Socialists, among other things, had called for the nationalization of banks, electric companies, telephones, telegraph, railroads, etc.

prices down; raise purchasing power. "For these things, too, and for a multitude of others like them, we have only begun to fight."

The old ghost, that 25 per cent spending cut, continued to haunt him. Wouldn't it be a good thing, thought FDR, to make another speech in Pittsburgh, scene of the original promise, justifying what he had said there four years earlier? He asked the loyal Sam Rosenman for a "good and convincing" draft of an appropriate speech. Rosenman re-read the first speech. He could imagine only one defense, he said.

"Fine," said FDR. "What sort?"

"Mr. President," Rosenman replied, "The only thing you can say about the 1932 speech is to deny categorically that you ever made it."

Instead, FDR went to Pittsburgh and admitted he had guessed wrong. "I ask you a simple question," he said. "Has it not been a sounder investment for us during these past three years to spend eight billion dollars for American industry, American farms, American homes and the care of American citizens?" Only a Republican die-hard could say "no."

Yet Alf Landon, amiable, honest, progressive Kansas governor, tried to find a way of saying it without alienating too many votes. Landon had made a small reputation by being the only Republican governor re-elected in 1934 and by balancing the Kansas budget. "I believe a man can be liberal without being a spendthrift," he said. The comment revealed the weakness in his attitude toward the New Deal. He could not attack Roosevelt's achievements in good conscience; he had supported them to the hilt in Kansas; all he could do was criticize the cost.

On three campaign swings by train Landon, tolerant, good-humored, confident, for some reason, of winning, spoke mild, reasonable words about prudent government. Perhaps his most memorable phrase was the one he coined at West Middlesex, Pa., his birthplace. "Wherever I have gone in this country, I have found Americans." He was a handshaker by nature; on the radio he stumbled, fumbled, and read cold speeches into the microphone; the electronic aspects of campaigning intimidated him, in contrast to Roosevelt, who slipped from one medium to another without dropping a vote.[11] They called Landon another Hoover, or, worse a "Kansas Coolidge;" and he bitterly resented the implication, though he could not say so.

On his fourth campaign swing Landon, sensing victory might elude him, exposed a bitter side to his amiable personality. Like Hoover, he said he was out to wage "a battle to save our American system of government." In one of the most intemperate campaign speeches on record, Landon said at Alberquerque that, "Franklin D. Roosevelt proposed to destroy the right to elect your own representatives, to talk politics on street corners, to march in political parades, to attend the church of your faith, to be tried by jury, and to own property."[12]

Some people must have believed Landon. A *Literary Digest* poll (using auto owners and telephone subscribers) gave the election to the GOP. On the basis of this poll, the North American Newspaper Alliance asked veteran Kansas editor William Allen White, a life-long Republican, for a Landon story to be released should he win. "You have a quaint sense of humor," White wired back. "If Landon is elected, I'll write you a book about him, bind it in platinum, illustrate it with apples of gold and pictures of silver, and won't charge you a cent. Why waste good telegraph tolls on a possibility so remote as the election of Landon?"

Nevertheless Republicans laughed at Jim Farley's prediction Roosevelt would lose only Maine and Vermont. Farley laughed last. FDR amassed 523 electoral votes to Landon's 8, which he

---

11. Jim Farley wrote that "the influence of the radio in determining the outcome of the 1936 election can hardly be overestimated." Without radio, said Farley, "the work of overcoming the false impression created by the tons of written propaganda put out by foes of the New Deal would have been many times greater than it was, and, to be candid, it might conceivably have been an impossible job."

12. Landon's 1936 program was entitled "The New Frontier." In 1961 in a TV interview Landon admitted the statement quoted above "seems a little exaggerated."

received from—glory to Farley—Maine and Vermont. The President won an incredible 60 per cent of the 44 million votes cast. Congress came back overwhelmingly Democratic as labor, immigrants, farmers, Negroes, and city people generally helped solidify the new majority party's strength, which, in 1936, clearly did not rest with automobile owners.

Twice more Roosevelt, his grip firm on American emotions, swept to unprecedented third and fourth terms in the White House. In 1940 he took on a younger, more streamlined, and more progressive breed of GOP challenger. Wendell Willkie, the tousle-haired apostle of modern Republicanism, swept the country like a reincarnation of William Jennings Bryan. He was a Wall Street lawyer and president of a big utility, the Commonwealth and Southern Co., but Willkie had been a Democrat most of his life and never held public office. He stampeded the Republican convention as a new face and a dynamic thinker; [13] now, continually disorganized, his pockets full of junk, his head full of ideas, his dark green campaign train with its 12 special cars full of enthusiastic political amateurs, he prepared to wage all-out war to overturn Roosevelt. At first Willkie spread the same gospel as Landon: there's nothing basically wrong with the New Deal, but I can do it better and cheaper.

Copying FDR's brain trust, Willkie had a special car full of lawyers and journalists to draft speeches en route. These he delivered in a home-spun way over a loudspeaker built into the rear platform of the last coach. Like Bryan, Willkie rested only on the

13. Willkie was the last candidate for President to hold a formal notification ceremony. He was "notified" of his nomination at Elwood, Indiana, his home town, before 250,000 people—probably the biggest political rally in history. "I lament its passing," said Joe Martin, the Republican congressman of the venerable ritual. "It not only stimulated political activity throughout the state in which it was held but also provided a rallying point for the party nationally." Of course, both parties have managed to rally the party in front of millions on television; today the old ceremony would not have much use.

Sabbath. He took his special train into backwoods America, hitting places no candidate for President had ever been before. By rail, air, automobile he traveled 30,000 miles in a near super-human effort to reach every voter in person. He spoke 540 times in 34 states, giving 10 and 12 speeches a day for days on end.

No Republican, no Presidential candidate, in fact, had ever done anything like it. Willkie grew hoarse and tired railing against FDR's violation of the "no third term" tradition, and of the concentration of power in one man's hands. "Willkie is losing his voice," joked FDR to his personal physician, Dr. Ross McIntire, at one point. "I think it would be a grand gesture on your part if you would get in touch with his doctors and offer them your own favorite prescription for treating such trouble. We've got to keep him talking."

While Willkie criticized the New Deal's failure to restore prosperity, the war in Europe had caused American factories to begin tooling up for defense. Congress passed a selective service act. FDR, immersed in defense problems, planned not to campaign. People knew him, he said. They would have to decide for themselves whether they wanted him a third time. When Willkie suggested a series of debates like those of Lincoln and Douglas, Secretary of the Interior Harold Ickes replied, "The President cannot adjourn the Battle of Britain in order to ride the circuit with Mr. Willkie."

Unable to join issue with Roosevelt, Willkie, like Landon and Hoover before him, resorted at the last to fear. He began talking in late October about "secret treaties" to drag America into the war. "We do not want to send our boys over there again," he said ominously. FDR's mail began to reflect concern that he was taking the country into war. Shaken by Willkie's success (even as he had once shaken Herbert Hoover), Roosevelt, 12 days before election, made the first of five last-minute radio addresses, assuring the nation no secret treaties existed.

Willkie continued to goad him mercilessly; at Boston, just before election day, Roosevelt made the pledge which, like that of his own "great chief" Wilson 24 years earlier, would always haunt him. "I have said this before, but I shall say it again and again and again," came the confident voice from a million radios. "Your boys are not going to be sent into any foreign wars. They are going into training to form a force so strong that, by its very existence, it will keep the threat of war far away from our shores."

With terrifying prescience Willkie lashed back at the President. Five months, he said, was the average length of time a Democratic pledge was kept. "On the basis of his past performances with pledges to the people," said the Republican candidate, "you may expect we will be at war by April 1941, if he is elected." Willkie missed by nine months. On December 7 the Japanese Navy attacked the American fleet at Pearl Harbor; the United States had embarked on World War II.

FDR could no more be held responsible for World War II than Herbert Hoover the depression or Lincoln the Civil War. All were cosmic events, their roots sunk deep in history; none could have been headed off by campaign pledges; all would have come regardless of the White House's occupant. Yet the need of the hour demanded reassurance; and the power to reassure was FDR's great gift. The President won by 5 million votes; 8 Mid-Western states alone joined Maine and Vermont in the Republican column.

Willkie represented an aborted attempt by some Republicans to recapture the sense of adventure of Teddy Roosevelt's time. He was a sort of internationalist Senator LaFollette, a maverick who stood for progress; but he was able to win the GOP nomination only because of his amateur standing. He had the right big business connections, but, like Hoover, he was clean, non-partisan, and perhaps (some thought) easily managed. To have sent an Old Guardsman against the New Deal would have been the worst folly. Willkie offered himself as a GOP compromise, a conservative who had some vision for the future.

Willkie fooled the party. The GOP had spent its middle age right up to the moment searching for a man untainted by entrenched Old Guard style politics who was not likely to rock the boat, shift the power balance, or try to remake the party. In other words, it wanted a man with the right image, but not too many commitments. Willkie had the image, but he also had principles, among them a belief in "one world" and a conviction that the New Deal gains were there to be conserved not reversed. This earned Willkie the "me too" stigma among the old party pros, who put him down as another wrong guess.

"I shall not campaign in the usual sense," said FDR, accepting a fourth nomination in 1944. "In these days of tragic sorrow, I do not consider it fitting." He decided on five speeches only, to be delivered close to Washington. He would reply to GOP attacks on his policies and innuendos about his health. To prove he remained hearty and fit despite the burdens of war, Roosevelt drove 50 miles through New York City in the rain before making one speech. Later, he gave his famous Fala address, wherein he protested "libelous statements about my dog."

Thomas E. Dewey, the Republican nominee, was by far the ablest candidate to run against Roosevelt. Trim, handsome, with a Clark Gable mustache, he had made a reputation as prosecutor of New York mobsters in the 1930's and won the governorship of New York in 1942. Dewey, like Willkie, represented a forward-look in the Republican party; but he was also a professional politician, adroit at intra-party manuever. What's more, he had a good radio voice. "If there be those among you who would turn back the course of collective bargaining," Dewey admonished his conservative backers, "they are doomed to bitter disappointment." He too accepted the New Deal. "We are not going back to anything, not to bread lines, not to leaf raking, not to settling labor disputes with gunfire and gas bombs . . ." The trouble, said Dewey, was that now the nation's progress was in the hands of "stubborn men grown old and tired and quarrelsome in office."

Fresh, young blood was needed said the 42-year-old-Dewey.

Dewey, too, took to the campaign train. But he kept his route secret and would not speak from the rear platform. He made short, direct, and carefully-phrased speeches from auditoriums and halls throughout the North and West. His target was the radio audience. His speaking voice—deep, resonant, enhanced by excellent diction—impressed all who heard it. Win or lose, Thomas E. Dewey was the kind of candidate who might be heard from again.

Republican orators, of course, continually threw up to Roosevelt what he had said "again and again and again" about keeping out of the war. On November 4, in a radio speech at Boston, he replied in his flawless style: "We got into this war because we were attacked by the Japanese—and because they and their Axis partners . . . declared war on us. I am sure that any real American would have chosen, as this Government did, to fight when our own soil was made the object of a sneak attack." Then, pausing significantly, he added, "As for myself, under the same circumstances, I would choose to do the same thing—*again and again and again.*"

The nation was not about to change captains in mid-passage. It returned the most popular President in history to the White House a fourth time. Dewey, however, received 99 electoral votes, 17 more than Willkie. Yet, in four campaigns against Roosevelt, the GOP won a grand total of only 248 electoral votes— not enough to elect one candidate.

Campaigning against FDR, the Republicans, fighting for survival, surrendered the tradition of aloofness. Like the post-Civil War Democrats, they hustled votes and solicited attention. Yet childhood memories lingered in the GOP subconscious, and conflict over party programs prevented the formulation of concrete national policies. So Thomas E. Dewey, the ablest GOP dragon killer since TR, would go out and lose again in 1948 not because he lacked the ability to win, but because the dead hand of his party's past grasped him around one ankle.

Chapter 10

"GIVE 'EM HELL, HARRY!":

HARRY S. TRUMAN

"A man who faces an uphill election fight will in very many cases do what Mr. Truman is doing; that is, he will pursue a type of campaign which his followers will call 'hard-hitting' and which his opponents will call 'irresponsible' or 'sensational' . . .

"Governor Dewey is acting like a winner. He can afford to disregard the charges of his opponents and by doing so appear on a higher plane of statesmanship . . ."—*The Wall Street Journal*, September 24, 1948.

"I'll give the Republicans the toughest fight they were ever up against," President Harry S. Truman told editor Grove Patterson, of the *Toledo Blade*, in 1948. "I'll go into every town of over ten thousand people in America," he said as he reeled off his campaign plans. Patterson was astonished. "The thing that made the situation fantastic," he wrote, "was that apparently not a man, woman, or child in the United States believed he could do it. His cabinet and party leaders had washed him up and checked him off."

The GOP had just nominated the popular Governor Thomas E. Dewey, of New York, for a second shot at the Presidency. Everybody agreed Dewey was as good as in. The New Deal had run its course; the Democratic party had lost its steam. The campaign of 1948 was looked upon as a ritual to ratify a foregone conclusion. The only factor no one bothered to write into the equation was Truman himself, and the tradition he represented.

Harry S. Truman had taken the long path to the White House. Born on a farm at Lamar, Missouri in 1884, he grew up in Independence where his father, at the turn of the century, was a successful grain speculator. In 1900 Harry got a job as page in the Democratic national convention at Kansas City. There he saw

Bryan, a boyhood hero, nominated for President the second time.
(Years later, after the invention of the loudspeaker, Truman recalled in amazement how Bryan had captivated 17,000 noisy
people without any help from a microphone.)

Young Truman pushed a plow for 10 years, worked in a bank, [1]
served in artillery in World War I, and returned to Kansas at age
35 to marry and open a small mens' wear store with a friend. The
store made money for a year, then folded when farm prices dropped in the Harding administration. Through his war buddies
Truman came to the attention of the Pendergasts, Missouri's ruling
family in the 1920's, and was soon a county judge. Earthy
sensible, friendly, warm, he did what he was supposed to do and
succeeded in politics. In 1934, with machine support, he won a
seat in the United States Senate; during World War II his investi-
gations of bungling in government contracts put his name in headlines. Seeking a Roosevelt running-mate acceptable to all factions
in 1944, the Democrats lit on Truman as the ideal compromise; he
didn't especially want to be Vice President; he liked the Senate
fine. But as a good party man, he felt bound to accept the honor.

In April 1945, hardly more than a year after the election,
Franklin Roosevelt collapsed and died of a cerebral hemorrhage
at Warm Springs. The world mourned; and Harry S. Truman,
small-time politician from Missouri, bewildered at his sudden
elevation, took the oath as 32nd President of the United States.
He inherited a world war and the intricacies of a peace settlement
to follow. The Allies were on the verge of the final push in Europe
against Germany. In the Pacific General Douglas MacArthur prepared to move against the Japanese islands. Truman soon had to
make the painful decision to drop A-bombs on Japan. The war's

---

1. When Truman, age 22, was in the bank, President Theodore Roosevelt passed
through Kansas City. He, who would not enter politics for 15 years, ran out "just to
see what a President looked like . . . I was disappointed to find that he was no giant,
but a little man in a long Prince Albert coat to make him look taller," he recalled in
his memoirs.

end found millions around the world in need of food, shelter, work. Again the great powers sat down to start a world organization, a United Nations, to pick up the pieces; America, still suffering Wilson's anguish, eagerly joined.

Truman grew into his job quickly. He outlined the Truman Doctrine to give aid to Greece and Turkey against Communist incursions. He backed the Marshall Plan to help Europe get back on its feet. At home his forthright civil rights message to Congress in 1947 cheered liberals; but also aroused the enmity of Southern Democrats, who would later form their own Dixiecrat (States' Rights) party and run Senator Strom Thurmond, of South Carolina, for President. Meantime, FDR's former cabinet member, Henry A. Wallace, had started a new Progressive party, which he hoped would attract liberals and former New Dealers. (Unfortunately for Wallace, it also attracted Communists, and this rebounded to Truman's advantage.) Republicans had won Congress in 1946, and passed bills over Truman's veto, notably the anti-labor Taft-Hartley law and an act to end price controls. With their great vote-getter FDR gone, the Democrats began casting about for another man the country could be persuaded to hold in similar affection. Their eyes fell on the popular hero of Europe, General Dwight Eisenhower, then President of Columbia University. No, said Ike dismissing a boomlet for his nomination, military men should steer clear of politics. [2]

Next, the Democrats tried to recruit liberal Justice William O. Douglas of the Supreme Court; when Douglas refused, the party was left with incumbent Harry Truman, the man whose programs had been bludgeoned to death in Congress by Republicans and Southern Democrats. The party was not happy with Truman.

---

2. "I could not accept the nomination even under the remote circumstances that it would be tendered me," wrote Ike to Leonard Finder, who had entered him in the New Hampshire primary. "The necessary and wise subordination of the military to civil power will be best sustained when life-long professional soldiers abstain from seeking high political office." It took four years for the GOP to convince the General to change his mind.

"We're Just Mild About Harry" read placards at the Philadelphia convention. "If Truman is nominated he will be forced to wage the loneliest campaign in recent history," declared columnists Joseph and Stewart Alsop. Nobody but Truman himself—as editor Patterson learned—believed Truman could win. Pollsters predicted a Dewey landslide; in July Elmo Roper said further polling would be a waste of time. So distinguished a pundit as Walter Lippmann had written off the President months earlier. The best the Democrats could hope for, said Lippmann, "is to survive as an opposition . . . There can be little doubt that a national ticket headed by Mr. Truman would be a severe handicap and perhaps even disastrous."

Meanwhile, the Democratic convention delegates started a squabble over civil rights. Southerners objected to a mild plank endorsing equal rights in vague terms and submitted a minority report stressing states' rights. Mayor Hubert Humphrey, of Minneapolis, running for the Senate, brought in a liberal minority report calling for fair employment laws, abolition of segregation in the armed forces, and laws outlawing the poll tax and lynching. The convention, much to Truman's surprise, voted for the Humphrey plank. Immediately 25 delegates from Mississippi and Alabama walked out waving a Confederate flag.

In an atmosphere of extreme un-enthusiasm the Convention nominated Truman on the first ballot. At 2 in the morning, of a sweltering July night the President strode jauntily to the rostrum to accept the doubtful honor of his disgruntled party. In contrast to the men below he looked fresh and confident in his neat business suit, white shirt, and natty bow tie. The photographers' flashbulbs sent sparks of light glinting from his eyeglasses as he placed a black notebook on the lectern. ("I had studied the acceptance speeches of two or three other Presidents, principally Roosevelt's," Truman would later write, "and I had made up my mind that I would spring my first big surprise of the campaign in that speech.")

Apathy hung like smog in the hot auditorium. Truman waited

for the feet to stop shuffling. He opened with a flat assertion he expected to win. He did not come to defend his record; it needed no defense. Instead, he launched into a slashing attack on he "do-nothing Republican 80th Congress." As the President jabbed away, a spark of interest flared. Some delegates sat straighter. He was going right back to Washington, he said, and call a special session of the 80th Congress. That was his bombshell. He would give the Republicans a chance to pass all the laws they said they were for in their platform, ratified in this same hall, just a few weeks before: anti-inflation laws: housing laws; a national health program; civil rights; increased minimum wages; extended social security.

"Now my friends," he said, picking up steam, "if there is any reality behind that Republican platform, we ought to get some action from a short session of the Eightieth Congress. They can do this job in 15 days if they want to do it. They will still have time to go out and run for office." Like a corpse rising from the coffin, the tired delegates stood and cheered. They stamped their feet. They whistled. The building rocked as the exhausted Democrats forgot, in the excitment of Truman's fighting speech, they had written themselves off. Truman, like Bryan in 1896, like FDR in 1932, had ignited a spark of hope with his dramatic acceptance. "I still don't think the Democrats can win the campaign," reported Martin Agronsky, "but whether he wins or loses, Harry Truman in one little speech . . . has lifted what was a beaten party up on its feet again and put it back in the campaign."

Truman's impulse to attack the Republican Congress had not come to him, like some Hebraic vision, in a dream. A month earlier he had crossed the country in an 18-car special train, ostensibly to collect an honorary degree from the University of California at Berkeley. Stopping at Chicago, Omaha, Carey (Idaho), Eugene (Oregon), and Spokane, the President turned the tour into a long critique of the 80th Congress. When he called it the "worst Congress" in history, the crowds cheered lustily. Truman knew he had found an issue, though no one else at the time, least of all the GOP, could see it. (Critics carped at Truman's trip in much the same language used on Stephen Douglas. "The President in this critical hour is making a spectacle of himself that would reflect discreditably on a ward heeler," said the *Washington Evening Star.*)

Once nominated, Truman knew exactly what he should do. "I want to see the people," he told his press secretary Charlie Ross. "I'm going to visit every whistle-stop in the United States!" His mission was considered as hopeless as Bryan's in 1896 and more so than Alf Landon's 40 years later. Truman was cast by the press and pollsters in the roll of an out-party candidate challenging a popular incumbent. "We were on our own 20-yard-line," said St. Louis attorney Clark Clifford, who led the Truman brain trust. "We had to be bold. If we kept plugging away in moderate terms, the best we could have done would have been to reach midfield when the gun went off. So we had to throw long passes . . ."

The incumbent Truman decided to do what his mentor Franklin Roosevelt had done in 1936; fight back from the stump. Where Roosevelt once flayed the "economic royalists," Truman attacked the "do-nothing 80th Congress." On Labor Day at Detroit he threw his first long pass, denouncing the Taft-Hartley law to 100,000 industrial workers. If a Republican becomes President, predicted Truman, "you men of labor can expect to be hit by a steady barrage of body blows . . . We are in a hard, tough fight against shrewd and rich opponents. They know they can't count on your vote. Their only hope is that you won't vote at all . . ."

This was not the "dire prediction" tactic of a desperate Hoover or Landon. Truman could cite chapter and verse. At Flint, Michigan, he borrowed an Al Smith technique to quote straight from Republican campaign literature. He had vetoed the tax cut bill, he said, because it cut national income but meant nothing to small wage earners. A $60-a-week employee received only $1.50 a week more under the bill; a $100,000 a year executive could count on $16,725 more each year. "Is it any wonder that we call this a rich man's tax bill?" Truman asked. "The Republican National Committee thought it was and undertook to collect."

The President held up a newspaper. "I want to read you something here that is just as interesting as it can be—I don't think I have ever seen anything as interesting. Now this is called *The Republican News*. It is the official publication of the Republican party . . .

"Here it is: 'Don't Throw Peanuts to the Elephant' (Laughter) Wait a minute—you will find out what the 'peanuts' means. Take a look: 'Many of our friends feel that, entirely apart from other important considerations, the least they can do to express their appreciation is to contribute a substantial part of their tax savings for this year to insure the re-election of the Congress which made this possible.'

"That is the terrible 80th Congress they are talking about that didn't do anything for the country," said the President.

On this first tour Truman also hammered this theme home at Grand Rapids, Hamtramck and Pontiac, where the great crowds and loud cheers were put down to labor sympathy for the memory of FDR. In one week the President had traveled 10,000 miles and delivered 75 speeches. It was the most intensive piece of campaigning an incumbent had ever done. Harry Truman considered it just a warm-up.

Back in Washington, he prepared for the main swing of his campaign, a 22,000 mile jaunt to the Mid-West and West Coast. At Union Station in Washington his armor-plated special car, the "Ferdinand Magellan," was made ready. Weighing 285,000 pounds, it had 3-inch-thick bullet-proof glass windows, a lounge, a dining area seating 12, four bedrooms, a galley, and a bathroom. It was hooked to a 17-car train of aides, speech writers, and reporters. "I'm going to fight hard," the President told his running-mate, Senator Alben Barkley, of Kentucky, as they shook hands in the station. "I'm going to give 'em hell!" Meanwhile, high officials

in the Administration had quietly put their Washington houses up
for sale.

Everybody knew Harry Truman could not win; but you had to
hand it to the plucky man with the horn-rimmed glasses and pug-
nacious jaw. He might be a loser, but he had guts. Enormous
crowds turned out to see him. The Republicans dismissed it as
curiosity. Everybody likes to see a President. At a little town
in Ohio, Frank Lausche, Democratic candidate for governor of
Ohio, emerged from a crowd of 6000. He had come reluctantly
to the train, hoping not to be contaminated by the President's
losing image. He agreed to do his duty and ride with Truman as
far as Columbus. As they neared the city the crowds swelled. So
many people jammed the railroad station hundreds had to wait outside on the pavement.

"Is this the way all the crowds have been?" asked Lausche in
disbelief.

Truman smiled. "Yes," he said, "but this is smaller than we've
had in most states."

"Well, this is the biggest crowd I ever saw in Ohio," said
Lausche, who decided he would accompany the President to Cleveland after all.

At every whistle-stop on his tour Truman poured on the coal.
The local band having played "Hail to the Chief" he would accept
a small gift with polite thanks. Sometimes he dedicated a factory
or an airfield. Often he introduced his wife Bess, "the boss," and
his daughter Margaret, "the Boss's boss," which never failed to
draw applause. Then he got down to business. Hands pumping
up and down, polka-dot bow tie bobbing, Harry Truman, in his
flat Missouri twang, gave 'em hell.

"They have already stuck a pitchfork in the backs of the farmers
by cutting down on funds for crop storage," he told an Iowa farm
audience. "I warn you, that's their real attitude. First the little
cuts, then all price supports will be thrown out." Not only farmers but wage earners and old people had suffered the indifference

of the do-nothing Congress. "As your President, I made every effort to get the Republican 80th Congress to extend social security coverage and increase social security benefits. What did the Congress do? They took social security benefits away from nearly a million people!"

Always it was attack, attack, attack. "Those fellows are just a bunch of old mossbacks . . . gluttons of privilege . . . all set to do a hatchet job on the New Deal." Of course that's not what his opponent said, Truman admitted. "The candidate," he confided, in a rare reference to Dewey, "says 'Me Too.' But the Republican record still says, 'We're against it.' "

At Louisville he took on the National Association of Manufacturers, which, he claimed, had spent $3 million to end price controls in 1946. Holding up an NAM newspaper ad, he read: "If OPA is permanently discontinued . . . prices will adjust themselves quickly to levels that consumers are willing to pay." Truman shrugged and smiled. "Prices adjusted themselves all right," he said. "They adjusted themselves the NAM way—the big business way—the Republican way—up and up and up. For instance, here in Louisville, you paid 28 cents for chuck roast in June, 1946. In August of this year you were paying 67 cents . . . These prices did adjust themselves—they doubled."

Dewey, meanwhile, campaigned like a President. Confident of victory, he drew about his shoulders the mantle of dignity, in the best McKinley tradition. Since Roosevelt no Republican dared shun the stump entirely. But Dewey's campaign train, the "Victory Special," moved at a leisurely rate, leaving out many whistle-stops. Dewey's cool, efficient, well-organized speeches were turned out in marathon sessions by a group of expert writers under the candidate's personal direction. They contained much good writing, but no concrete policy statements. "We know what kind of government we have now," Dewey would say with a sigh, never mentioning Truman by name. "It's tired. It's confused. It's coming apart at the seams. It cannot give this nation what it needs most—what is the real issue of this election—unity."

Dewey said everything beautifully, but nothing specific. Joseph W. Martin, Jr., the Republican House leader, advised his candidate to defend the excellent record of the Congress from Truman's scathing attacks.[3] When Dewey visited North Attleboro, Massachusetts, even Joe Martin's old mother, who had seen many candidates come and go, admonished him, "Don't take it so easy." Though he had been a two-fisted slugger running for governor of New York, Dewey now chose aloofness. Everyone said he was as good as President. He would act the part. He would preserve the image.

At Chicago Truman aimed a low blow calculated to shake Dewey's imperturbability. He likened the Republican candidate's mustache to Adolph Hitler's. Dewey immediately sent wires to Republican state chairmen around the country. Did they think he could take the gloves off and start punching? No, said the professionals, don't spoil it. "They all agreed," said a GOP speech writer, John Franklin Carter, "that the proper thing for Dewey to do was to ignore Truman's personal attack and continue along the high road to the White House."

Even the high road had its detours. At Beaucoup, Illinois, Dewey's train, without warning, backed up into the crowd. Though no one was hurt, people ran screaming in all directions. "That's the first lunatic I've had for an engineer," Dewey remarked. Truman, hearing about it, used the comment to needle the Republicans. "He objects to having engineers back up," said the President. "He doesn't mention that under that great engineer, Hoover, we backed up into the worst depression in history."

---

3. Martin's view of the 80th Congress contrasted somewhat with Truman's. "The Marshall Plan, Greek-Turkish aid, the Taft-Hartley Act, tax reduction, the first balanced budget in 17 years, unification of the armed forces . . . the 22nd Amendment, the presidential succession bill, the Hoover Commission, expansion of the Voice of America—these and many other substantial measures made the 80th a particularly constructive and progressive Congress." Dewey was not willing to go so far.

Still unperturbeded, Dewey arose late each day, and delivered his calm, reasonable, dignified, vague speeches. At the Rushmore Memorial in South Dakota, one reporter commented Dewey "spoke like a man who already guided the nation's destiny." And another newsman quipped, "How long is Dewey going to tolerate Truman's interference with running the government?" In all 107 speeches Dewey gave not the least clue he believed himself to be in a hot fight for the Presidency. He moved airily around the country. He played the same dates Truman did, often to much smaller crowds, a fact to which nobody seemed to attach much meaning. Dewey shared the national delusion he had already won.

"Tom Dewey has returned to Albany every inch a President," reported the New York *Daily Mirror* early in October. "The major campaign trip is over, almost 9000 miles, coast-to-coast and back again, fifteen days of constant travel meeting and speaking with the people whom he will serve for four years beginning January 20th, assuming that no miracle occurs in the meantime."

In the meantime, the miracle-in-the-making, Harry Truman, worked as zealously as a prohibition orator in a local option fight. He averaged 10 speeches a day for 35 days, becoming, incidentally, the first presidential candidate to stump among Harlem's Negroes. The man was seeking the office; he made no pretense about that. Winding up at Madison Square Garden the President repeated that he did not doubt he would win. "I have had a consultation with the White House physician," he told the crowd, which grew still and sober at these words. "I told him I kept having this feeling that wherever I go there's somebody following behind me. The White House physician told me not to worry. He said, 'You keep right on your way. There's one place that fellow's not going to follow you, and that's into the White House!' "

The day after election Truman was photographed at the St. Louis railroad station holding up an early edition of the Chicago *Tribune*. "DEWEY DEFEATS TRUMAN" read the banner. The President was smiling. He had received 24 million votes to Dew-

ey's 22 million, 303 electoral votes to 189. He had won almost
as handily as FDR in 1944. It was an unprecedented feat. "Mr.
President," read a sign on the front of the Washington *Post* newspaper building, as Truman rode up Pennsylvania Avenue, "we
are ready to eat crow whenever you are ready to serve it." Columnists, analysts and pollsters fell all over each other in the rush
to explain why they had been so wrong.

Thousands of people, it is thought now, couldn't decide how to
vote until election day. Many of them said they went into the
booth planning to vote for Dewey and emerged having pulled
Truman's lever. An Iowa farmer who came from the Dakotas in
1932 with $2.85 in his pocket now had a 160-acre farm, a herd of
cows, a new Plymouth and a bank account. "I talked about voting
for Dewey all summer," he told opinion analyst Samuel Lubell,
"but when the time came I just couldn't do it. I remembered the
depression and all the good things that had come to me under the
Democrats."

Indeed, Lubell believes many farmers voted for Truman be-
cuse they saw him not as a wild, experimental New Dealer—the
New Deal, after all, was 16 years old—but as the *more* conservative
candidate. He had said exactly where he stood on permanent flexible price supports for farm crops, expanded soil conservation programs, better roads, more farm co-ops, extension of electricity to
farms. Dewey's vague and polished platitudes made farmers uneasy. "Why change when the Republicans were so speculative?" an
Iowa minister asked Lubell. Dewey had promised to clean house.
"What would be swept out with the housecleaning?" the minister
went on. "Price supports and other agricultural aids? If another
depression somes, what will farmers do?"

Truman's bitter attacks on the Taft-Hartley law also drew factory workers to the polls who might have stayed home in apathy.
As a rule, no incumbent President campaigns by saying, "If I'm
elected I will do this or that." If he does, he invites Will Rogers'
question: "How come you haven't done it already?" Truman

headed off this query by shifting the onus to Congress. He tried to raise the minimum wage, he said; the 80th Congress thwarted him; he tried to extend social security coverage; he tried to get a housing program. Give me a Democratic Congress this time, he pleaded, and I will get the bills passed.

Truman found it was not as easy to get action as he thought. Between 1948 and 1952 he succeeded with public housing, social security, and increased minimum wages; but aid to education and health insurance failed. Congress tightened up the farm price support program, moved to conserve soil and control floods, and expand the rural electrification and public power programs. In foreign affairs, a bi-partisan area which had not figured much in the campaign, Congress renewed the reciprocal trade agreements, ratified the North Atlantic Treaty Organization, and extended the Marshall Plan. On the other hand, the Republican-Southern coalition blocked civil rights and all attempts to revise the Taft-Hartley Act.

In 1949 there was a furor when the Communists took over China and forced Chiang Kai-shek to Formosa. Both parties in 1950 supported Truman's decision to send troops to the defense of South Korea; but the Democratic majority in Congress was cut severely in the 1950 elections. Senator Joseph L. McCarthy was abroad in the land, hunting Communists, and his main target was the State Department and its head Dean Acheson. Some minor scandals turned up in the Bureau of Internal Revenue and the Justice Department; though well below the magnitude of the Harding era they offered the Republicans a potent campaign issue for 1952. The Democratic hold on its natural majority had slipped.

Running against Truman in 1948 Dewey acted out a party memory of a time when candidates avoided issues and kept their "dignity." He behaved like an incumbent, not a challenger—McKinley in 1900, TR in 1904, or Hoover in 1932—ignoring partisan flurry and keeping as high above the battle as he could. Dewey's strategy might have worked against a Democrat equally preoccupied with image. But in this century there has never been a Democrat like that. Image or not, Democratic candidates have dealt in substantive matters, of bread and butter, war and peace.

Dewey shunned specific policy statements, while Truman cited chapter and verse in his indictment of the 80th Congress. Each man operated within the framework of a party tradition, and Truman, for all his lack of polish, got the better of it. In retrospect there was no reason to think a political descendant of Bryan, Wilson, Al Smith, and FDR would lie down and lose just because the newspapers said he was finished.

Chapter 11

THE GENERAL AND THE PR MEN:

DWIGHT DAVID EISENHOWER

"I'll talk about the burden of taxes and their dangers to a people's initiative, but let me tell you—I'll be darned if anyone is going to talk me into making any idiotic promises or hints about elect-me-and-I-will-cut-your-taxes-by-such-and-such-a-date. If it takes that kind of foolishness to get elected, let them find someone else for the job."—Dwight D. Eisenhower, quoted by Emmet John Hughes in *The Ordeal of Power*, 1963.

Voice: "Mr. Eisenhower, can you bring taxes down?"
Eisenhower: "Yes. We will work to cut billions in Washington spending and bring your taxes down."—Radio-TV spot announcement, Citizens-For-Eisenhower, 1952.

In 1952 "the most admired living American," according to a Roper poll, was General Dwight David Eisenhower. His appeal transcended hero worship. The intense blue eyes, benevolent face, ruddy cheeks, and broad grin conveyed accessibility, magnetism, and great warmth. Schooled in war, he symbolized peace. Innocent of politics, he seemed capable of beating politicians at their own game to win the White House not for self, not for party, but for everybody.

Like George Washington, Eisenhower despised petty intrigue, pompous oratory and phony ballyhoo. No man had wanted less to be President. For the GOP, capturing Ike was a feat worthy of Frank Buck. Senator Henry Cabot Lodge revealed in January 1952 that Eisenhower would accept a Republican draft. In Paris the General, then head of NATO forces, confirmed Lodge's statement; but he insisted he wasn't a candidate. "Under no circumstances will I ask relief from this assignment in order to seek nomination to political office," he said, "and I shall not participate

in the pre-convention activities of others who may have such an
intention with respect to me."

Within months Eisenhower had resigned his post, returned home,
solicited Republican convention delegates, and made speeches for
himself. Duty, not the Republican party, he was convinced, had
called him back; the people had rewarded a lifetime of service by
asking him to serve once more. His integrity could end corrupt
partisan government; his dedication to peace could restore national
purpose. The nomination for President would be his vehicle, but,
unfortunately, politics being what it is, he would have to ask for the
job.

No, Ike told reporters, he had not changed his views since 1948,
when he refused flatly to run. An "overriding reason" compelled
his campaign. "I am certainly going to try to work honestly,
honorably and in keeping with what I really believe the American
people would like me to do," he said. "In doing so I run into
many things that disrupt personal plans, personal aspirations . To
my mind that is of no moment . . . I don't want to lie to you and
say that I love all his . . . I do say that I'm in it now with heart and
soul . . ."

As George Washington longed for Mt. Vernon, so Ike preferred private life to the Presidency. Aloof, non-partisan, above
politics, the General was an antidote to the Truman scandals and a
tonic to the squabbling GOP. There never was a Republican candidate like Eisenhower. His nomination produced a spectacle unique
to campaign history: a man too forthright for partisan sham, too
honest for pedestrian deception, impatient of deals and manuever,
chasing votes with techniques so blatant any party pro would blush
to think about them.

Not only did the General whistle-stop, shake hands, work the
cornfields and shopping centers, and make 300 speeches; he delivered station-break television commercials for himself. Not only
did he attack the Democrats where they were most vulnerable; he

made vague promises very like the ones he vowed not to make. The most remarkable thing is he got away with it. Somehow the Eisenhower image—man-above-politics, everybody's candidate— emerged untarnished. Other than Washington himself, it is hard to imagine any nominee who might have enabled the GOP to discard so completely the tradition of aloofness. Eisenhower could do anything. It would never be labelled "politics."

On the strength of this image Ike won the Republican nomination. The GOP in 1952 was split roughly along the same lines it had been for 40 years. Favorite son of the Old Guard, or Mid-Western isolationists, was "Mr. Republican," Ohio's Senator Robert A. Taft. Taft, the humorless but utterly sincere son of a President, had co-authored the Taft-Hartley Act (against which Truman campaigned so effectively in 1948). As keeper of the conservative conscience, he stood for reduced spending, a balanced budget, and limited government. The Old Guard, understandably, had had enough of "me too" candidates who looked like Republicans but sounded like Democrats. "We followed you before and you took us down the road to defeat!" intoned Senator Everett Dirksen as he pointed a finger at Thomas E. Dewey in the 1952 convention. Taft, like Barry Goldwater, believed that voters given a "real" choice, would assert their grassroots conservatism in favor of the GOP.

The Dewey group of Eastern liberals,—which included Lodge, Herbert Brownell, and Sherman Adams—rejected Taft's premise. But intraparty animosity remained so high the liberals could not hope to dictate to the convention a candidate who shared their politics. They were castaways on a sea of hostility; Ike would be their life raft. "The tantalizing appeal of the Eisenhower candidacy," wrote Samuel Lubell, "was that of a clean sheet of paper, free of all the bitter repetitive partisan scrawling of the past."

At Chicago's Blackstone Hotel, Eisenhower, stage-managed by Brownell, shook hands with delegates, posed for pictures with

party hacks, and bestowed upon one and all the gift of his famous
grin. Meanwhile, his managers shrewdly contested the seating of
some Southern delegates and charged Taft had tried to "steal" the
nomination. Their self-righteous scorn, televised to the nation,
forced capitulation on the Taftites. Eisenhower was nominated
on the first ballot. George Washington had beaten the grubby
politicians. Young Richard M. Nixon, a California senator who
had made a reputation as an anti-Communist in the Alger Hiss case,
became the General's running-mate in a gesture to regional balance
and party harmony.

Eisenhower called for a "Great Cruside" in his acceptance
speech. "Our aims—the aims of this Republican crusade—are
clear: to sweep from office an Administration which has fastened on
every one of us the wastefulness, the arrogance and corruption in
high places, the heavy burdens and anxieties which are the bitter
fruit of a party too long in power."

To Ike this was no mere political campaign. It was a battle.
"Before this I have stood on the eve of battle," he said. "Before
every attack it has always been my practice to seek out our men in
their camps . . . and talk with them face to face . . . In this battle
to which all of us are now commited it will be my practice to
meet and talk with Americans face to face in every section, every
corner, every nook and cranny of this land." He would not be a
politician after votes, but a leader marshalling his troops to over-
come the forces of evil.

Superficially the campaign, with its trains, motorcades, press
conferences and speeches, looked like the Democratic invention
every Republican had emulated since 1936. Eisenhower discussed
foreign and domestic policy on the radio and television. He attacked the Democrats and promised to change things if elected.
What made his campaign unique, however, was the manipulation
of the candidate's image. It was impossible to think of Eisenhower
as a Republican. He could not really see himself that way if, by

Republican, one meant party politician with a partisan program.[1]
The secret of Ike's appeal was in his nonpartisanship. Where
politicians pretended to be for peace, home, mother, God and
country, Eisenhower really was. He had no political, social or
economic program to trade for votes. He had only his transcendent
goodness. So the candidate himself for the first time, had to be
packaged like a commodity in such an attractive way voters would
hustle down to the corner polling booth and pull his lever on election day. Ike's lack of political experience became a virtue. He offered the electorate not just an alternative to Democrats, but to
politics itself: a President untainted by the wards, courthouses,
legislatures, and backrooms of America.

Only a "clean-slate" could have lent itself so aptly to the growing
use of public relations in politics. Candidates for lesser office
had employed PR men before. The Presidency was something else.
A politician running for President Madison Avenue style had to be
careful; he could be cut to ribbons by the opposition for trying to
manipulate votes in a manner unbecoming the nation's highest office. Not General Eisenhower. Instead of the PR techniques degrad-
ing the candidate—and history, tradition, and precedent supported
the belief they should—Ike lent dignity and prestige to the techniques.

The Democratic candidate, Adlai E. Stevenson, did not share
Ike's judgment that politics and public service were contradictory.
Grandson of a Vice President, he had grown up in a home swirling
with political talk. He was just as reluctant to run for President
as Eisenhower, but for quite different reasons. A Chicago lawyer
known for his wit and dignity, Stevenson in 1948 had been elected

---

1. Wrote Sherman Adams, "As a candidate and as President . . . Eisenhower had
a strong aversion to engaging in partisan politics. A high-minded idealist, he had
assumed that the Republicans had nominated him mainly because they wanted a
President with his wartime and NATO experience who stood the best chance of
bringing permanent peace to the world. It came later as a grim disillusionment when
he realized that many of the Old Guard Republican leaders were really using his
prestige and popularity only to wrest political power from the Democrats."

reform governor of Illinois; now he aspired to a second term to finish projects barely under way. "One does not treat the highest office within the gift of the people of Illinois as a consolation prize," he said.

Stevenson would not lift a finger to further his own candidacy. Unlike the world-famous Eisenhower, he was barely known outside of Illinois. He had told President Truman early in 1952 he could not accept the Democratic nomination. He was still saying "no" that summer when, on the third ballot, his party chose him over Senator Estes Kefauver and W. Averell Harriman, of New York. Ike believed candor and politics incompatible; Stevenson, in the Woodrow Wilson tradition, considered one the essence of the other. He would, he said in his acceptance speech, "talk sense to the American people . . . tell them the truth, that there are no gains without pains . . . Better we lose the election than mislead the people; and better we lose than misgovern the people . . .

"And the Democratic party is the people's party, not the labor party, not the farmers' party, not the employers' party—it is the party of no one because it is the party of everyone." He looked upon the campaign as a "great quadrennial opportunity to debate issues sensibly and soberly . . . not as a crusade to exterminate the opposing party . . . "

Meanwhile, Eisenhower, had expressed comparable sentiments —though not in public. "All I can hope to do in this or any other campaign," he told Emmet John Hughes, on leave from Time, Inc., to help draft speeches, "is to say what *I* believe. And this does not mean always getting in wrangles and scuffles with the other fellow . . . The people who listen to me want to know what *I* think—not what I think about what someone *else* thinks. This is all I have to offer. If the people believe in what I say, and do, nothing else matters—and they will vote for me."

Nevertheless, a great public relations and advertising machine was assembling to put words, ideas and beliefs into the General's mouth. Robert Humphreys, head of the GOP's public relations

division, served as coordinator, working with commercial advertising agencies like Batten, Barton, Durstine & Osborn. Under
Humphreys' supervision an elaborate Campaign Plan was drawn
for the GOP. It described where the votes were, why the Democrats had got most of them in the past, and what the Republicans
would have to do to improve their score in 1952.

The Plan was read to Ike and his managers at Denver's Brown
Palace Hotel in August. For the first time the General began to
see how he fit into the party's strategy. It was assumed the GOP
had about 20 million "natural" votes, based on the Willkie and
Dewey returns in three elections. These voters, many of them conservative Mid-Westerners, to whom Ike's nomination had been
interpreted as a rebuke, "must not be alienated." The implication
was that Eisenhower must make peace with Taft.

Out of an estimated 90 million eligible voters, the "me too"
independents amounted to no more than 5 per cent. To court
them as Dewey had done was folly. They were too few to matter.
The real potential GOP strength, said the Plan, was among 45
million "stay-at-homes," the people who only came out when
agitated. It would take massive anti-Democratic propaganda on
the radio, on TV and in the newspapers to get them to the polls.

"The whole spirit of a campaign conducted on this level," the
Plan said, "would be one which could inspire a crusading zeal
that is impossible to engender by the 'me to' approach, or anything
which promises only to better what the present Administration is
doing . . . the recommended strategy is: "Attack! Attack! Attack!"

The Plan also sketched the marketability of the GOP's main product—its candidates—and the sales pitch and media. "Both Republican candidates have warm and winning personalities," it said
of Ike and Nixon. "Both have a high degree of salesmanship in
their manner . . . Obviously the thing to do is to gain entrance for
them into the homes of America by every means possible so that
the warmth of their personalities can be felt." Television was the
ideal medium "to make the most of the ticket's human assets."

Furthermore, station-break spot announcements would be " a *must* for stimulating the voters to go to the polls and vote for the candidates." It had not been decided yet who should deliver the spots.

Nor did the Plan outline issues. It was a matter of "merchandising Eisenhower's frankness, honesty and integrity, his sincere and wholesome approach," said Bernard C. Duffy, president of BBD&O. The operation seemed strangely like a paraphrase of Bryan's free silver declaration in 1892: The people trusted Eisenhower; therefore the Republicans offered Eisenhower; they could look up the reasons later.

During the briefing, the General sat silent. Sherman Adams sensed he was annoyed and later asked him what the trouble was. "All they talked about was how they would win on my popularity," said Ike in a flash of insight. "Nobody said I had a brain in my head."

But the General did what was expected. His September meeting with Taft at Morningside Heights in New York strained the credibility of his claim to aloofness; yet it did him no harm, even with those liberals who had thought his nomination to be a rejection of Taft's politics. Over breakfast the nominee and Mr. Republican found more in common than either had suspected. "I wished to be sure that the new administration will be inspired by the philosophy of extending liberty before I entered into an extensive speaking campaign," said Senator Taft. "After a satisfactory discussion with General Eisenhower this morning for two hours, I am satisfied that is his philosophy . . . I think it is fair to say that our differences are differences of degree." Ike, like the amiable Harding, seemed to have the knack of making all factions believe his real sympathies lay with *them*. He accepted the idea that to unify a nation he would have to unify his own party first. Quipped Adlai Stevenson, "It looks as if Taft lost the nomination but won the nominee."

Eisenhower undertook the most ambitious whistle-stop tour in Republican history. Where the GOP used to write off the South automatically, the General spent more time below the Mason-Dixon line than any candidate since Stephen Douglas, visiting every state but Mississippi. Nor did he neglect the rest of the country. He traveled 40,000 miles in all, by train and motorcade, in 34 states. On its face the campaign looked much like the Bryan-Wilson-FDR stump tour; behind the scenes, however, the stage management smacked more of Winfield Scott. For Ike had not come to talk politics, an area remote from his experience or taste. He was on a Great Crusade, to be enlivened by his warmth, earnestness, nonpartisan sympathy, stamina, and famous grin.

No detail of the tour was left to chance. "And each of his stops," wrote Stanley Kelley, Jr., "was accompanied by what was probably the most meticulously planned and sustained ballyhoo yet shown in a presidential campaign tour." The Eisenhower entourage was preceded by an advance man who visited each town on the route to insure newspaper, radio and TV coverage. Then a task force of crowd-builders, "Young Industry for Eisenhower," would follow to get up a telephone campaign, and recruit cheerleaders to throw confetti by the ton and give out campaign buttons and rally invitations.[2] Ike's crowds, on the strength of his world stature, could have been expected to be large; under the build-up, they proved enormous and uniformly enthusiastic.

No detail of planning was too small for ad men used to getting maximum mileage from every dollar. A 39-page blueprint, for example, was written just for Ike's opening appearance in Philadelphia's Convention Hall. It specified "fresh cut roses (25,000) ... noisemakers (3000) ... flags (5000) ... programs (25,000)." It included the specific instruction that Ike, at Independence Hall must stand so as to be photographed with his right hand on the Liberty Bell.[3]

---

2. Vice-presidential candidate Nixon received similar detailed planning services. Murray Chotiner, his manager, drew up a 125-item blueprint for Nixon's appearances—including the patriotic touch that a Korean veteran, if available, should always be called upon to lead the pledge to the flag.

3. Those interested in the role of the PR man in politics will find Stanley Kelley, Jr.'s book *Professional Public Relations and Political Power* (from which many of the above details are taken) enlightening.

However, the most elaborate planning was reserved for the radio and TV-spot announcements. The idea for TV spots by the candidate instead of formal speeches had been proposed to Dewey in 1948 by a soap company executive. Dewey, confident of winning anyway, draped in the mantle of dignity, rejected it. Four years later a group of interested Republicans approached Rosser Reeves, of the Ted Bates ad agency, for a slogan to counteract the Democrats' "You Never Had It So Good." "If you want to elect Eisenhower," he replied, "you go after maximum penetration: use spots."

Reeves volunteered to plan a spot campaign; he asked a former Bates producer, Michael Levin, to do the preliminary market analysis and sales pitch. Levin—basing his conclusions on Lubell's *The Future of American Politics*—decided the Republicans could win by switching 49 key counties in 12 states to Ike. The spot campaign should consist of an "all-out saturation blitz" of these counties by radio and TV in the last three weeks of the campaign.

And so Eisenhower, who had no intention of making "any idiotic promises or hints," was eased, by the back door into a role he had never envisioned for himself. "The spots themselves would be the height of simplicity," Levin wrote. "People from each of the 49 areas would each ask the General a question . . . The General's answer would be his complete comprehension of the problem and his determination to do something about it when elected. Thus he inspires loyalty without prematurely committing himself to any strait-jacketing answer. This was a technique that Roosevelt certainly employed, and was certainly successful . . ." [4] The GOP, at long last, would use Democratic techniques. The plan suggested a budget of $2 million for spots alone; about $1.5 million was eventually spent.

Through Walter Williams, of Citizens-for-Eisenhower, this conception was presented to Sherman Adams and Ike and accepted by

---

4. FDR's technique was the vague promise, not the spot announcement.

both. Reeves set out to write the scripts. His research required the reading of old Eisenhower speeches in back newspapers. What was Ike's main theme? "He was talking about three thousand things," Reeves told writer Martin Mayer. "And you don't do that in advertising. You lose penetration." From the jumble Reeves picked a dozen ideas. These he took to public opinion analyst Dr. George Gallup who put his finger on three themes that had people worried: the Korean War; corruption in government; taxes and the cost of living.

On production day Reeves joined Eisenhower at the Transfilm Studios in New York City with 22 scripts. Ike, reading from hand-lettered cards, proved a fast worker; so Reeves, who planned to take a few days to do 28 more scripts, sat down at a typewriter in a backroom and banged them out on the spot. Each was passed to Ike's brother, Dr. Milton Eisenhower, for final approval. Meanwhile a Bates executive lettered the cards, and a camera crew stood by. Ike had not thought to veto the spot idea any more than the pre-convention delegate hunt, any more than the whistle-stop ballyhoo, any more than his political philosophy as rendered by Senator Taft. Now he permitted Reeves, with Gallup's help, to decide for him what he believed and should say. Maybe the incongruity struck him. Between takes, Martin Mayer wrote, the General sat grimly in a hard-back chair shaking his head and muttering, "To think that an old soldier should come to this."

The spots were not scheduled for release for more than a month; in the meantime there were set speeches to make; the Republicans had three themes now: Corruption, Communism, Korea. The first concerned the Truman scandals; the second was based on charges of subversives in government; the third held that the Truman administration had either started, or prolonged, or mishandled (it was never clear what) the Korean War. In radio and TV speeches, at whistle-stops, in great halls around the country, Ike elaborated these themes. He ably carried out the Republican strategy of "attack". At Philadelphia, for example, he hit corruption: "This

Washington mess is not a one-agency mess or a one-bureau mess
or a one-department mess—it is a top to bottom mess . . . stirred
into this sorry brew are all the facts you have learned and many
more none of us will ever hear about—of Washington waste and
extravagance and inefficiency . . . "

Not as rabid as Nixon or Senators McCarthy and Jenner on
Communism, the General still got in his licks: ". . . we will find the
pinks; we will find the Communists; we will find the disloyal."
At Milwaukee, in deference to McCarthy's sensibilities, he deleted
a paragraph praising his good friend General George C. Marshall
whom McCarthy had charged with turning China over to the Communists. The charge was preposterous, and Ike knew it; yet he
bowed to the politicians. As for the Korean War, he asserted it
resulted from "a failure to build up adequate strength in Korea's
own defense forces." He had not yet decided on a personal visit.
On welfare, Ike ducked the "me too" charge by simply removing
the issue from politics. He would neither repeal nor extend the
New Deal; its gains were past debating. "Social security, housing,
workmen's compensation, unemployment insurance, and the preservation of the value of savings—these are things that must be
kept above and beyond politics and campaigns," he said. "They
are *rights* not *issues*." How FDR's ghost must have chuckled over
that statement from a GOP candidate.

In the last three weeks the main themes were hammered home in
the radio and TV spots. Ike's face, in some areas, appeared on
television several times an hour. (In New York alone 130 spots
were broadcast the day before election.) For the Republicans
had pre-empted (at a fat price) commercial time on regularly
sponsored shows. A show ended; then, instead of the usual plug
for soft drinks, or soap, or toothpaste, a solemn voice said: "Eisenhower answers the Nation!" The dialogue went like this:

Man-in-the-Street: "Mr. Eisenhower, what about the high cost
of living?"

Eisenhower: "My wife, Mamie, worries about the same thing. I tell her it's our job to change that on November 4th."

Or, to take another example:

Man-in-the-Street: "Mr. Eisenhower, I need a new car but can't afford it at today's high prices."

Eisenhower: "Yes, a low-priced car today includes $624 in hidden taxes. Let's start saving the billions now wasted by Washington and get those taxes down."

Reeves even worked in an antidote to the Democratic slogan that had brought him into the campaign:

Man-in-the-Street: "General, the Democrats keep telling me that I never had it so good."

Eisenhower: "Can that be true when America is billions in debt, when prices have doubled, when taxes break our backs, and we are still fighting in Korea? It is tragic. It is time for a change."

Democratic reaction to the spots was emphatic and negative. George Ball, of the Stevenson camp, called the campaign "a super-colossal, multi-million dollar production designed to sell an inadequate ticket to the American people in precisely the way they sell soap, ammoniated toothpaste, hair tonic or bubblegum." Nevertheless a Democratic ad agency executive admitted the only reason his team hadn't used spot saturation was lack of funds. In fact, the Democrats did spend a small amount of money ($77,000) on spots. In one of them, for example, a voice said, "Sh-h-h-h. Don't mention it to a soul, don't spread it around . . . but the Republican Party was in power back in 1932 . . . 13 million were unemployed . . . bank doors shut in your face . . ." However, the Democratic candidate never delivered this propaganda himself.

Stevenson, laboring under the handicap of anonymity, made good his promise to talk sense and speak truthfully. To get around the country he relied more on the airplane than any candidate had before. Of the 32,500 miles he covered, 27,140 were by air; his use of the rear platform was confined mainly to a trip from Chicago to New York and back again in the waning days of the campaign, when, according to the reporters, he began to draw crowds nearly as large as Ike's.

Balding, slightly paunchy, with a manner of quiet reserve, Stevenson—in contrast to the ruddy, robust Eisenhower—did not stand out in a crowd. People would sometimes applaud his manager Wilson Wyatt, mistaking him for the candidate. But when he spoke, Stevenson threw sparks. As John Mason Brown observed, Ike's inner light and great warmth somehow went dead during a speech. With Stevenson, the reverse happened, and it was "as if a giant switch were thrown on and Stevenson's personality and strength blazed forth in their full light." The Democratic candidate repeatedly stressed his belief a campaign ought to consist of enlightened discussion of public policies, of dialogue between the candidates, of national soul-searching by voters. His ideas mirrored Wilson's (he had attended Princeton), and his 1952 speeches reminded many listeners of the 1912 Democratic candidate.

No master plan buttressed the Stevenson campaign. Except for the substitution of planes for trains, it was much more traditional than Ike's. The candidate would decide what he wanted to say; it was up to his aides to decide where and when he should say it. His publicity staff consisted mainly of newspapermen; they improvised techniques as they went along; the Democratic advertising agency, The Joseph Katz Company, was retained mainly to buy time and space for routine speeches and ads, and to produce campaign literature.

Stevenson's speeches were written to make people think. He refused to hedge any issue. To an American Legion audience, for example, he remarked he would "resist pressure from veterans, too, if I think their demands are excessive or in conflict with the public interest . . ." Reviewing Southern history at Richmond, Virginia, he restated his support for the strong Democratic civil rights plank. "I should justly earn your contempt if I talked one way in the South and another way elsewhere," he said. At Portland he told newspapermen he wished "that the newspapers so highly agitated over the two-party system in politics would contemplate the very real dangers of the one-party system in the press." He was especially dismayed that most papers had "rushed to commit themselves to a candidate last spring, long before they knew what that candidate stood for, or what his party platform was, or what would be the issues of the campaign." [5]

Stevenson tried hard to start a meaningful debate on foreign policy. He expressed a belief in co-existence and competition between the USSR and the West until such time as the United Nations could put the world on some more secure basis. (Ike, by contrast, made uncertain remarks about how the United States should help the satellite nations to "liberate" themselves from "Soviet Tyranny." He never said how.) Stevenson's wit became legendary. On one occasion, noting that the platform Ike spoke from in Richmond (as Bryan always feared after his Yale experience) collapsed, Stevenson quipped: "I'm glad the General wasn't hurt. But I wasn't surprised that it happened— I've been telling him for two months that nobody could stand on that platform." Another time, when his voice came echoing back at him in a vast town square he observed, "I think what I am saying is worth listening to, but it's certainly not worth listening to twice." At Bakersfield, California, he offered, "If the Republicans will stop telling lies about us, we will stop telling the truth about them."

Although Stevenson made many sardonic jibes at his own expense, the ones aimed at Ike soon drew return fire. "It would be very, very fine if one could command new and amusing language, witticisms to bring you a chuckle;" said the General. "The subjects of which we are speaking these days . . . are not those that

---

5. Ike had the support of 993 papers with 40 million readers against 201 papers and only 4.4 million readers for Stevenson. In nine states there was not a single Stevenson paper.

seem to me to be amusing . . . Is it amusing that we have stumbled
into a war in Korea; that we have already lost in casualties 117,000
of our Americans killed and wounded; is it amusing that the war
seems to be no nearer a real solution than ever; that we have no
real plan for stopping it?   Is it funny when evidence was discovered that there are Communists in government and we get cold
comfort from the reply, 'red herring'?"   GOP, said Stevenson,
after Ike's sally, must now stand for "Grouchy Old Pessimists."
He could never engage the General to talk about the issues in long-
range policy terms.

Meanwhile the campaign produced an unexpected crisis that
nearly wiped out the carefully-drawn Republican plans. A group
of California businessmen, revealed columnist Peter Edson, had
given Richard Nixon $18,000 in a "secret fund" to offset his ex-
penses as a United States Senator.   Republicans as well as Democrats demanded Nixon's resignation from the ticket.   Instead, the
Senator, availing himself of television, decided to take his case to
the people. BBD&O bought $75,000 worth of air time for the
night of September 23. Nixon planned a speech that would not
only exonerate him in the fund matter but stir more support for
the party. "This broadcast must not be just good," he wrote afterwards. "It had to be a smash hit—one that really moved people . . . " To build suspense he kept secret even from his wife
and managers what he intended to say. "I determined . . . I must
do nothing which might reduce the size of that audience," he recalled.

Ike, meanwhile, campaigning in the East, decided to suspend his
judgment until Nixon could make his defense and the public's
response be assessed. The broadcast proved Nixon a cool performer
in an extremely ticklish situation. His fund, he said earnestly, was
not secret; no money went for his personal use; no favors were
granted in return for contributions. In a firm voice he recited his
life story—the poor boy who had worked his way through college,
married, gone off to war, returned to practice law and run for

Congress. He listed everything he owned—from a 1950 Olds-
mobile to GI life insurance, and paid homage to his wife's "respectable Republican cloth coat."

In nine million livingrooms (half the TV sets in the country),
Americans nodded in sympathy as Nixon bared his life, his fin-
ances, his affection for the wife and daughters flanking him on
stage, and the family's affection for another gift they had received,
a black and white cocker spaniel named Checkers. ". . . I just
want to say this, right now, that regardles of what they say about
it, we are going to keep it."

The fund story, said Nixon, was a smear cooked up by his political enemies. They had been bruised by his attacks on Communism.
No matter. He would do nothing to hurt Dwight Eisenhower's
chances for election. The decision to keep him on the ticket lay
with the Republican National Committee. He urged viewers to
register their preferences without delay. As he walked, perspiring,
from the stage, there were tears in the eyes of the cameramen; they
did not cry alone. Nixon's "Checkers speech" had been witnessed
by an estimated 60 million people, the largest TV audience in history. He had displayed to them a "degree of salesmanship" never
envisioned by the Republican Campaign plan. Between one and
two million letters and telegrams demanded Nixon be kept on the
ticket. "If it hadn't been for that broadcast," Nixon reflected, "I
would never have been around to run for the Presidency."

Ike's response was characteristic. "Dick, you're my boy!" he
said, embracing his running-mate who had flown to meet him in
West Virginia. A deliberate "father-son" imagery was conjured
up in the relationship of Nixon to Eisenhower, said Kenneth
Davis, a biographer of both Ike and Stevenson. "When the son
got into trouble . . . father forgave him," Davis wrote, and "the
whole episode became classic-American, of a piece with George
Washington's telling *his* forgiving father that he'd done it with his
little hatchet."

Nowhere was the image of Ike-as-father more potent than in his celebrated Korea promise 10 days before election. It had been conceived for him by Emmet John Hughes, and written into a speech without Ike's prior knowledge. "To bring the Korean War to an early and honorable end" was his first aim, said Ike at Detroit. "That job requires a personal trip to Korea. I shall make that trip. Only in that way could I learn how to best serve the American people in the cause of peace. I shall go to Korea."

In five words Eisenhower crystallized the emotional symbolism of his campaign. More than the spots, more than the attacking speeches, the Korea promise pinpointed the kind of magic people believed Ike could perform. "We knew it was right long before Eisenhower delivered it," said Sherman Adams. "When mimeographed copies of it were distributed to reporters on the train, they said to us excitedly, as soon as they saw the 'I shall go to Korea' line, 'That does it—Ike is in!' "

Stevenson's camp reacted with a sour grapes statement that their man had talked—privately—about doing the same thing for months. Their comment missed the point of Eisenhower's candidacy. A promise by the governor of Illinois to visit Korea would have invoked little symbolism. Only a military hero, known to be commited to peace by his intimacy with the arts of war, could imply so much with a simple pledge. "The statement," said its creator Hughes, "was for him, natural and appropriate, almost to the point of being banal." But it sharply focused public longing for an end to conflict and magnified Ike's stature even more.

Not all of Eisenhower's campaign promises proved so specific or susceptible to fulfillment. Just before election he reiterated his 10 main pledges. He would, he said:

    —be President of "all the people," regardless of race, creed or political party;

        —take no steps to repeal "social gains" made by either party;

        —restore "integrity and competence" to government;

        —fight inflation;

—eliminate wasteful government spending and take steps toward a reduction in taxes;

—defend the workingman "against any action to destroy his union or his rights" (amending Taft-Hartley was implied), and promote fuller employment and higher wages;

—support farm prices at present levels;

—work to make "equality of opportunity a living reality" for all Americans;

—engage in no "witch hunts or character assassinations" but strive to "prevent infiltration of Communists and fellow travelers" into government;

—make "peace in the world for ourselves and for all free people" the primary goal of foreign policy, and start by going to Korea.

To wind up the campaign BBD&O produced a spectacular one-hour TV show at a cost of $267,000. It purported to be a documentary "report" to Ike on the potency of the Great Crusade as he sat watching with friends in his livingroom. With this production, the single, dramatic election-eve speech of the candidate from his home town, seemed to become a relic from Model-T days. BBD&O took viewers through 81 changes from film to live broadcast, from San Francisco, to Los Angeles, to Seattle, to Cleveland, to Philadelphia, and Boston. A kaleidoscope of people, places, impressions, events rushed the campaign to its climax—workers at Lockheed, Oveta Culp Hobby, Nisei for Eisenhower, author Louis Bromfield, whites, Negroes, old people, and the 10-year-old organizer of Tykes for Ike. The whole world, it seemed, was backing Eisenhower. In one sequence a Korean vet, stopped on the street by an announcer, looked into the camera and said, "Well all the guys I knew out in Korea figure there's only one man for the job, General, and that's you."

The vet's sentiments squared precisely with those of 34 million other Americans—nearly 10 million more than had elected Harry Truman in 1948. Ike received 55 per cent of the popular vote and a whopping electoral majority of 442 to Stevenson's 89. He won Democratic states like Virginia, Florida, Texas, Oklahoma, and Tennessee, and started serious talk of a two-party South. Despite his concessions to the ultra-conservatives McCarthy and Jenner, Ike ran well ahead of them too in their own states. He might have done even better had he conceded nothing at all.

The Republican party's first victory in 20 years was not the result of a voter consensus on issues. It was not even the fruit of the imaginative public relations campaign. General Eisenhower, hero, man above politics, did not need to be sold like soap. His name, reputation, integrity, evident sincerity, sunny smile—these qualities spoke well enough for themselves. It seems ironic that the man who least needed it allowed himself to become associated with PR gimmicks no professionl politican—running for President—would have tried.

As it turned out, the Republican Campaign Plan, brilliant as it seemed, was wrong in important details. Stay-at-homes stirred by attack did not give Ike his stunning majority. It came from people who voted Democratic in 1948 and decided a change to Eisenhower—not Republicanism—would be a change for the better. If Ike had run as a Democrat against, say, Robert A. Taft, it is hard to imagine the result would have been different. Nor did the TV speeches and spot announcements tip the balance. Most people made up their minds long before the spot campaign. A study at Miami University (Ohio) concluded that in 1952 "any influence of television could not possibly have been of a decisive nature. The results apparently would have been the same with or without this new, and as yet untested means of political communication."

By electing a man "above party" the nation got what it bargained for in Ike. But the new President had a hard time getting what he bargained for in GOP unity. The same Republicans who bucked his candidacy thwarted his legislative program in Congress. Ike went promptly to Korea—that was easy; and he worked out a truce, though no peace treaty was forthcoming. Where promises required the help of Congress, though, they proved harder to keep. The legislators would not amend the Taft-Hartley Act. Lower, flexible farm price supports replaced the previous rigid program and made Secretary of Agriculture Ezra Taft Benson notably unpopular.

Despite Ike's pledge to eschew "witch hunts," the witch-hunting Senator McCarthy made considerable mischief in the federal government without public protest from the White House. Not until he tried to move in on the United States Army was McCarthy brought to heel and censured in the Senate. As for the budget, despite its pledges, the GOP could not balance it either; the national debt continued to rise. And though Congress put money into foreign aid and mutual security it cut the President's request each year.

There were some plusses. The Administration secured a tax cut and the first revision of the federal tax code in 75 years. Congress raised the minimum wage from 75 cents to a dollar. Though no civil rights legislation was proposed, the Justice Department argued with success before the Supreme Court against segregated schools, which were banned in 1954. Eisenhower's "anti-subversion" bills outlawing the Communist Party passed with bi-partisan support. Congress voted to extend social security to 10 million people.

The key word in the Eisenhower years was "moderation," and the President defined his course as "middle-of-the-road." He assiduously pursued peace. His "open skies" proposal to the Russians at Geneva in 1955 reflected a real concern with ways to ease the cold war, the main task for which he believed he was elected. Despite a heart attack in 1955 and stomach surgery in 1956 Ike was renominated. Despite the Democratic take-over of Congress in 1954 his popularity remained phenomenally high. Opposing Adlai Stevenson again in 1956 the President, an incumbent now, was inclined to keep his campaign activity to a few televised speeches. Yet enormous pressure was put on him (mainly by local politicians still enamoured of the coat-tail theory) to travel, speak, and support Republicans everywhere. At the end of September he made a West Coast trip; along the route eager crowds chanted "We Like Ike," as the kindly, confident President beamed down upon them. At Pittsburgh, Senator Duff, of Pennsylvania, introduced him with the not-too-original accolade, "First in war, first in peace, first in the hearts of his countrymen." Yet the phrase embodied an emotional truth. It fit no man since Washington better than Dwight Eisenhower.

As the first GOP President in 20 years Ike was necessarily his party's leader; but he could never see himself as a partisan politician. "*This* is what I mean to people," he told Emmet Hughes, holding up a newspaper editorial in the 1956 campaign. "Sense and honesty and fairness and a decent amount of progress. I don't think the people *want* to be listening to a Roosevelt, sounding as if he were one of the Apostles, or the partisan yipping of a Truman. This business of rolling the drums to rally your own party troops has its place, but—damn it—everyone that comes into this office tells me that *I* am the only thing can pull this party through. So there's no use my making any compromises with the truth . . ."

Ike never recognized any of his campaign activities as a "compromise." His heart was pure, therefore his actions, whatever they seemed, must likewise be pure. In 1956 Ike gave no television commercials; and Stevenson, exhausted by a primary fight with Senator Estes Kefauver, struggling, without succeess to associate the President with the Republican party, abandoned much of his earlier candor and wit. No weapon seemed adequate to the potent good-will, recuperative powers, and non-partisan determination of the symbol in the White House.

Neither Eisenhower nor Stevenson produced even the seeds of a policy debate in 1956. "Each candidate defined his position in terms so general that it became almost impossible to distinguish it from that of his opponent," wrote Stanley Kelley, Jr., who added that "the campaign was in large part repetitious assertion of ficti-

tious 'issues.' " As so often in the past, the President's attention
was diverted by the unforseen. A week before election Israel
attacked Egypt in the Sinai Peninsula and the French and British
began bombing Egyptian airfields in a drive to regain the Suez
canal. Ike called off his last-minute campaign trip plans, but
assured the nation the United States would not become involved in
the war. On November 6, rallying behind the first-in-war-first-in-
peace President, the nation re-elected Ike by a landslide. He received 457 electoral votes to Stevenson's 73, and 35.5 million popular votes against 25.7.

In most places Eisenhower's vote ran heavier than in 1952. He
picked up Kentucky, West Virginia and Louisiana, losing only
Missouri from his 1952 sweep. But for all Ike's popularity, the
Republicans could not drag in other candidates behind him. Winning the Presidency by 10 million votes, Eisenhower lost both
houses of Congress—a feat unprecedented in modern times. For
peace and moderation, voters seemed to say, they liked Ike. For
prosperity the Democrats, of whom there was still a voting majority, would stick to their own party.

Eisenhower broke a Democratic monopoly on the White House;
he did not succeed in realigning a majority of voters for his party.
What is remarkable about Eisenhower—in the perspective of
campaign history—were the concessions he made to compromise
the "dignity" of a presidential candidate without compromising
in the least his own image as a man-above-party. With Eisenhower
a wheel had turned full circle—from the aloof candidate who
itched so hard to win he kept quiet and let his managers run things,
to the aloof candidate who, in order to serve reluctantly, would
utilize every campaign technique ever invented and a few more
besides. No candidate in history defied the tradition of aloofness
as successfully as Dwight Eisenhower.

Campaigning for President Ike, more often than not, gave in
to expediency. He said he would stay in Europe in 1952, but came
home to chase the nomination; he vowed he would say what he

believed, but he cut out a reference to his friend General Marshall in a speech; he said he would make no promises he could not fulfill, but he delivered TV commercials for himself. He said he stood for the people above party, but he tried—without success—to lend his image to Republican candidates unfit to sit on the same platform with him.

Hero, idol, father figure—everything but politician—Ike made it possible for Republicans to ballyhoo their way at long last into the White House. Neither he nor his supporters could find it in their hearts to impute any narrow motive to anything he did. For the same reason, nobody could accept the Eisenhower program as a form of Republicanism. In electing Ike the nation rejected politics, GOP as well as Democratic. As a result, his election did not unify the Republican party; after eight years in power the GOP was no nearer a program all factions could agree upon than it had been in 1952. Neither the Taft-Goldwater nor Dewey-Rockefeller Republicans emerged as the dominant shapers of Republican policy while Eisenhower was in the White House. When the party returned to a political candidate for President, it chose, inevitably, Richard Nixon, the perfect mirror for its diversity of viewpoints.

Chapter 12

THE GREAT DEBATE:

KENNEDY vs. NIXON

"I am not going to begin by saying to those who are Republicans in this audience, 'Vote for me because I'm a Republican.' I believe that when we select a President of the United States that our history tells us that the American people look not just to party labels. They look behind them. They look to what he stands for, and they try to determine what kind of leadership America needs . . ."—Richard M. Nixon, streetcorner speech, 1960.

"One of the reasons why I am glad to come to Michigan is because I am running with distinguished, vigorous, progressive Democrats. One of the great things about being a Democrat is you don't have to do what Mr. Nixon does, who keeps saying that parties don't mean anything . . . I am a Democrat every day of the year, and I run as a Democrat, and I run in the succession of Woodrow Wilson and Franklin Roosevelt and Harry Truman. Mr. Nixon is the intellectual heir to McKinley, Dewey, Landon, Coolidge, Harding, Taft and the rest."—John F. Kennedy, streetcorner speech, 1960.

Averaging four hours sleep a night the last week of the 1960 campaign, John F. Kennedy spent Monday in Pennsylvania, Tuesday and Wednesday in California, Thursday in Arizona, New Mexico and Texas, Friday in Ohio and Virginia, and Saturday in New York. He had traveled 5000 miles weekly for three months. Now, sagging, tired, his right hand bruised from the pressure of countless palms, he rode in a motorcade through the Connecticut darkness. About 30,000 people—an incredible crowd for 3 o'clock in the morning—shouted as he pulled up to the Roger Smith Hotel in Waterbury. Election was two days off. On the balcony the weary candidate thrust his chin forward for one more speech.

"My name is Kennedy and I have come to ask for your support," he said. He made the usual gestures—praise for Connecticut, a joke on himself, criticism of his opponent. But in this impromptu talk he also quoted Tom Paine ("the cause of America is the cause of all mankind"), and Franklin Roosevelt's second acceptance speech ("Better the occasional faults of a government living in the spirit of charity than the consistent omissions of a government frozen in the ice of its own indifference.")

Governor Abraham Ribicoff made a short speech, then Kennedy returned. "I will close," he said, "by telling you of a letter which Lincoln wrote in a campaign very much like this, one hundred years ago, when the issues were the same. He wrote to a friend, 'I know there is a God, and I know he hates injustice. I see the storm coming and I know His hand is in it. But if He has a place and a part for me, I believe that I am ready.' Now, a hundred years later, when the issue is still freedom or slavery, we know there is a God, and we know He hates injustice. We see the storm coming, and we know His hand is in it. But if He has a place and a part for me, I believe that *we* are ready."

Kennedy, in contrast to Richard Nixon who rarely quoted any-body, often repeated the words of the first Republican President. He seemed to be attracted by Lincoln's sense of destiny and of his own limitations. History, to Kennedy, was an endless highway from the past into the future. He never lost sight of his place on the road, and he tried to communicate it to others. Partly this was the Kennedy personality; but in the long stream of time Kennedy's party had produced a number of Presidents with more than a cas-ual interest in the past. Wilson had been a historian and political scientist, Roosevelt a dabbler in naval history, and Harry Truman, who never went to college, is still a student and writer of American history. Was it just coincidence these were the names Kennedy invoked time and again in the 1960 campaign?

One hundred years after Lincoln opposed Douglas, there re-mained a Democratic and a Republican style of running for President. Kennedy's campaign was like a flashlight, charged by the past, illuminating the future. Nixon's seemed more like a mirror. Lacking rootedness—the days of McKinley and Teddy Roosevelt were too far distant—it could only reflect the GOP's present tensions and conflicts. Neither Barry Goldwater, whose tap roots ran back to the elder Lodge and Robert Taft, nor Nelson Rockefeller, TR's political heir, could get enough support to be nominated. Each man's views were so crystal clear—and antithetical—the GOP would sooner dissolve than unify around one of them. Aside from a happy image like Eisenhower, only a Nixon, whose ideas were flexible enough to shift with the party's winds, could expect to get support from the GOP liberals and conservatives.

Nixon's candidacy in 1960 makes a much more interesting case study than Kennedy's. He was the inevitable result of a party which for 50 years had been running in two directions at once and couldn't break the habit. Maybe Nixon could have won in 1960. He came very close in the popular vote. But, like Dewey, the GOP tradition could supply him with no useful precedents. Like the Democrats of 1860, the Republicans had stopped winning in 1932; so Nixon had no continuity of program or policy he could call his own. He had nothing to offer in exchange for votes. Where Dewey had taken refuge in the tradition of "dignity" in 1948, Nixon, inevitbly, ended up chasing an elusive image too. Perhaps he didn't realize it, but his 1960 campaign became an imitation, even a parody, of 1952 and Dwight Eisenhower.

There were some important differences, too, But the fact remains Ike had the winner's image. In 1960 Nixon tried to borrow it, and he failed because he remained, at bottom, a GOP party pro. Ike's great charm was that he was a-political. He offered the voters an alternative to politics on a program of self-righteousness. Nixon tried to prove his spiritual ancestor was Eisenhower and that, as Ike's protege, he had eight years of on-the-job training. But it was impossible for him to shake the party label.

Kennedy, with the instinct of a political animal, spotted Nixon's

vulnerability. He never let the GOP candidate forget his antecedents. "I stand in direct succession to Woodrow Wilson and
Franklin Roosevelt and Harry Truman," he said on a hundred
street corners. "Mr. Nixon, the Republican leader, stands in
direct succession to McKinley, to Coolidge, to Hoover, to Landon,
to Dewey." He didn't mention Ike at all.

Though Democrats had a five to three edge in voter registrations,
Kennedy's youth and Catholicism seemed bound to work against
him. On paper, Nixon had the edge. Though both men had entered Congress together in 1946, and both had served in the Senate,
it was Nixon who had been Vice President for the past eight years.
He had traveled in Europe, Asia, and South America; pictures of
him wagging his finger in Khrushchev's face had been printed all
over the country. He had successfully mediated a steel dispute.
When Ike took sick, the Vice President ably presided over meetings
of the Cabinet.

Still, the GOP had not gone wildly enthusiastic at the prospect
of nominating Nixon. Ike's endorsement had been lukewarm;
Nelson Rockefeller kept himself available. In the end Nixon inherited the job not so much because he was Ike's heir apparent as
because his political flexibility left him the only man able to unite
Old Guard and Eastern liberals. Nixon passed the acid test in the
tense debates over the party platform.

The mildly liberal Charles H. Percy, president of Bell & Howell,
chaired the Republican platform committee. Percy stood for a
modern, streamlined GOP. Most of the other platform writers,
however, leaned no farther left than Barry Goldwater. The committee wrote a conscientious, moderate platform. "Don't you see,"
one member told author Theodore White, "in this party you have
to run as hard as possible to stay in the same place; getting them
to approve what Eisenhower has already done is an achievement
in itself."

Rockefeller, the liberals' conscience, rejected the draft platform. He felt it was too weak on civil rights and national defense.

Threatening a floor fight, he summoned Nixon to his New York apartment for a secret conference. Next morning Rockefeller released the famous "Fourteen Point Compact of Fifth Avenue." It called for new Western alliances, an end to nuclear testing in the atmosphere, new underground tests, strong nuclear retaliatory power, more bombers and missiles, executive reorganization, an aggressive civil rights stand, federal aid to schools, and a voluntary medical care program.

In Chicago the GOP platform committee read about the meeting in the newspapers, and the members yelped like skinned cats. Goldwater called it "the Munich of the Republican Party." Even Eisenhower shared the sense of betrayal, for the 14 points included his own pet idea on reorganizing the executive branch. He had hoped to spring it in his last message to Congress.

Having satisfied Rockefeller, Nixon now flew to Chicago to bind up the wounds and stop the flow of conservative blood. One by one he talked to the platform committee members, telling them why he couldn't hope to make a good race without strong planks on civil rights and national defense in particular. Backing "aggressive action" on behalf of Negro voting, housing, schools, and jobs, Nixon fixed his sights on Negro votes in the big industrial states. Yet he softened the plank's language, in a gesture of harmony toward the conservatives. The word "sit-in" specifically was removed, and the final plank supported "the Constitutional right to peaceable assembly or resort to economic boycott."

After a hot debate, the Nixon-Rockefeller plank carried. Nixon had appeased the liberals, headed off a floor fight, and managed to placate Southern conservatives. The latter group, unhappy about the civil rights plank, were still grateful for the changes in wording, which would make their task of building up the GOP in the South less hard.

The Nixon-Rockefeller summit was a symbolic re-run of the Taft-Ike breakfast of 1952. Nixon became the broker between the GOP's conflicting wings and proved himself equal to the task of

making them flap in harmony. When Rockefeller, having had his
way on the platform, withdrew as a candidate, the convention
quickly chose Nixon. He picked Henry Cabot Lodge, former
Massachusetts senator, as his running-mate.[1] Lodge, the American
ambassador to the United Nations, and Nixon, the world-traveler,
made a formidable team in foreign policy.

Many considered the Vice President's acceptance speech his
best in the campaign. Lean, erect, serious, he told the GOP delegates in the Stockyards Amphitheater that speaking the truth about
the cold war would be the President's hardest job, "difficult because
at times our next President must tell the people not what they want
to hear but what they need to hear. Why, for example it may be
just as essential to the national interest to build a dam in India as
in California.

". . . When Mr. Khrushchev says our grandchildren will live
under Communism, let us say his grandchildren will live in freedom.

"When Mr. Khrushchev says the Monroe Doctrine is dead in the
Americas, we say the doctrine of freedom applies everywhere in the
world."

Nixon vowed he would "carry this campaign into every one of the
fifty states." Within 10 days his plane had taken him from Rhode
Island to Hawaii, stopping in Illinois, Nevada, California and
Washington state. It was the start of the most energetic assault on
the Presidency a Republican had ever made.

Kennedy, meanwhile, had taken the hardest path to the nomination. He won it in the primaries. Since 1956, when he had lost
the Vice Presidential nomination by a handful of votes to Estes
Kefauver, Kennedy believed the 1960 nomination to be within his
reach. His brother Robert, a 30-year-old lawyer, found a spot
for himself in 1956 as liaison between Stevenson's campaign plane

---

1. In 1952, while Ike was beating Adlai Stevenson by 200,000 votes in Massachusetts,
Lodge lost his Senate seat to John F. Kennedy by 70,000 votes, in part, some say,
because the Taft conservatives took a walk.

and national party headquarters. "Nobody asked me anything, nobody wanted me to do anything, nobody consulted me," Robert Kennedy later recalled. "So I had time to watch everything—I filled complete noteboks on how a Presidential campaign should be run."

Kennedy's age (44) was considered tender for a President; but his chief handicap was his religion. Since 1928 many people believed no Catholic could win. Kennedy entered the primaries to prove otherwise, and upset popular Hubert Humphrey first in Wisconsin, then in West Virginia, a state with a neglible Catholic vote.

Now Kennedy was hard to stop. To an interviewer he quoted Eisenhower's comment, "Being President is a very fascinating experience—but the word 'politics'—I have no great liking for that." Kennedy smiled. "I do have a great liking for the word 'politics,'" he said. Some measure of his liking was the personal machine he built to gain the nomination. It included lawyers, professors, political aides, and—not least of all—his sisters, his cousins and his aunts.

The Kennedys had a file of 20,000 cards, from which they could instantly pull data on nearly any Democratic politician in America. The name, address, job, religion, hobby, and first ballot choice of each convention delegate was recorded. They knew whether the delegate and Kennedy's office had exchanged letters, and which members of the family or staff may have met him. At the convention, 40 Kennedy liaison men watched every delegation, turning in reports daily to a "secret room" where four ladies updated the card files with current delegate strength.

Of all the aspirants—including Lyndon Johnson, Stuart Symington, and Adlai Stevenson—only Kennedy had his own telephone switchboard. Lines ran to the convention floor, to the candidate's Hollywood apartment, to the Biltmore hotel headquarters, and to a command post in a cottage behind the Los Angeles Sports Arena, where the convention was in progress. Kennedy workers watched the floor on television from the cottage. By phone or walkie-talkie they kept in touch with managers Robert Kennedy and Abraham Ribicoff. This explains the apparent coincidence some TV viewers noticed that each time a Stevenson or Johnson man visited a delegation, a Kennedy soon followed.

Should a delegate be overheard talking about deserting JFK, word was relayed to the secret room. There, his card was pulled and the data phoned to, say, Robert Kennedy, on the convention floor. The younger Kennedy might then approach the man, shake his hand, call him by name, remind him of some past association with the candidate, and, if possible, convince him to stick. The system proved so effective that Bobby Kennedy, on the first ballot, predicted within one-half vote the point at which his brother would be nominated.

The Kennedys in convention were a microcosm of the Kennedys in campaign. They emphasized teamwork, attention to details, tactics related to strategy. But JFK did not operate in an ideological vacuum. The platform committee, under Chester Bowles, had written the party's longest and most liberal document. Kennedy approved it and ran on it. To ease the blow of a strong civil rights plank upon Southern sensibilites, however, he picked Senate Majority Leader Lyndon Johnson, of Texas, to run with him. The choice had historic consequences.

As a speaker, Kennedy strove for understatement. Accepting the nomination he outlined, in a flat New England voice exhausted by the primaries, his call to action. In it, he acknowledged his political ancestry, as he would often do in the weeks ahead.

"The times are too grave, the challenge too urgent, the stakes too high to permit the customary passions of political debate," said Kennedy. " . . . Today our concern must be with the future. For the world is changing. The old era is ending. The old ways will not do . . . The problems are not all solved and the battles are not all won—and we stand today on the edge of a New Frontier—the frontier of the 1960's—a frontier of unknown opportunities and perils—a frontier of unfulfilled hopes and threats . . .

"Woodrow Wilson's New Freedom promised our nation a new political and economic framework. Franklin Roosevelt's New Deal promised security and succor to those in need. But the New Frontier of which I speak is not a set of promises—it is a set of challenges. It sums up, not what I intend to offer the people, but what I intend to ask of them. It appeals to their pride, not their pocketbook—it holds out the promise of more sacrifices instead of more security. . ."

In Washington, D. C., Richard Nixon watched the Kennedy speech on television. He considered it a poor job—too fast, too high-flown in language—and he observed that in a television debate he felt sure he could win.

Kennedy's strategy called for the hardest campaigning in the big industrial states—New York, Pennsylvania, Ohio, Illinois, New Jersey, and Nixon's own California. Lyndon Johnson, whose drawl became more noticeable the closer he got to the Gulf of Mexico, would be relied upon to woo and win the South. Later in the campaign Kennedy decided to concentrate upon the Republican suburbs of Northern Cities, trying to reduce Eisenhower's margins among young voters. As a Democrat, he believed he could win back minority group members—Negroes, Catholics, Jews—who had swung for the non-partisan Eisenhower.

Nixon opened his campaign in the South. He drew immense crowds in Georgia, North Carloina and Alabama. For a Republican it was a heady feeling. Did Ike's image have some carry-over after all? Nixon, commited by his strong civil rights plank to a pursuit of Northern Negro votes, began to wonder whether the South might be his too. To win both was to win the election. The dilemma reflected his party's inner tensions. Nixon had no Johnson to court the Democrats of the old Confederacy. He would have to do it alone.

The ambivalence that made Nixon an inevitable candidate clouded his relations with Ike. No one had more respect, even awe, for the President's powers as a vote-getter. But the son was unwilling to trade, overtly at least, on the famous father's popularity. "All we want out of Ike," a Nixon aide confided, "is for him to handle Khrushchev at the UN and not let things blow up there. That's all." [2] But was it? In his book *Six Crises* Nixon wrote that he understood Eisenhower would make his own decision on how and when to campaign for the ticket. "If the party people force him to make political speeches before he believes he should," General Wilton B. Persons told Nixon, "he simply can't put his heart into them . . . After Kennedy, Johnson, Stevenson and some of the other Democrats start to get rough he'll get his dander up and go after them." Ike did not join in the campaign until the last week. Meantime, he and Nixon had almost no contact with each other.

Not only was the potent resource of Eisenhower's image lost for much of the campaign, but Nixon, in his uncertainty, failed to use other party resources. He had, for example, two winning GOP campaign staffs from the Ike years at his fingertips. One, a Republican Plans Board, had been set up in Washintgon to schedule the candidate's moves. Nixon was supposed to meet the Board every week and make no decisions without consulting its members. After four meetings, he severed contact. "You could have taken the key to the Republican National Committee, locked the door, thrown the key into the Potomac, shipped all 175 employees off to the Virgin Islands and saved money—for all he ever listened to us," a member complained to Theodore White.

Where Ike, the man above politics, consented to all sorts of TV gimmicks, Nixon, the politician, ignored his television advisers too. In 1960 the Republicans set up their own ad agency, Campaign Associates, under Carroll Newton, BBD&O vice president. Nixon's TV adviser, Edward A. Rogers, was among the owners and more than 50 of New York's top agency people joined the staff.

---

2. Khruhschev had arrived in New York in September, called for the resignation of Dag Hammarskjold as Secretary General of the United Nations, the formation of a three-man secretariat and the admission of Red China. He performed his legendary shoe-banging act in the General Assembly on October 12 and left New York next day much to to the relief of both candidates.

Newton and Rogers proposed five special shows (i.e. "Khrushchev as I Know Him," with live comment, film clips of the kitchen debates and Moscow meetings). Nixon let the ideas dangle. Between July 25 and October 25 the agency staff stewed in New York while their candidate did not appear on one show controlled by the GOP alone.

Nixon seemed to fear being charged with dealing in "images." He ducked the imputation his campaign was created by ad men. In fact, he insisted the TV staff take offices on Vanderbilt Avenue in New York instead of Madison Avenue, the ad man's alley one block west. Nixon seemed to mistake techniques for issues, fearing to use what was available lest criticism be made not of what he was saying but how. Ike escaped this dilemma because he was convinced his own program was good for America no matter how it was presented. Nixon, as mediator of Old Guard and Eastern liberals, had no program he could be sure of. He bogged down worrying about images.

Nixon seemed to distrust outside advice too, relying instead on his own instinct for politics. He had, said the Eisenhower brain-truster Emmet Hughes, "the unshakable faith that he was, in an almost unique and surely superior sense, a 'professional' politician, loftily surveying a scene cluttered with 'amateurs.'" Yet, Hughes commented, he lacked confidence in most other things, and his own staff members pointed out how badly he could play politics at times.

Nixon's distrust of reporters, for example, became legendary. In the newspaper world it is axiomatic most publishers are Republicans and most reporters Democrats. Nearly 8 out of 10 newspapers supported Nixon in 1960; yet he refused to try to engage the sympathy or intellect of the newsmen themselves. Asked to attend an editors' meeting in Washington or New York, Nixon might say, "What for? They're all against me, anyway." Sometimes he barred reporters from his campaign plane. Theodore White spent weeks with the Nixon entourage taking notes for his book *The Making of the President 1960.* Yet, he reported, "it was impossible, despite repeated and persistent effort, to meet or talk with Mr. Nixon privately or discuss his campaign with him." At least half the reporters favored Nixon at the start, said White; nearly all were hostile at the end, fighting to keep their personal feelings out of their stories.

Nixon's views were a mixture of old Republican free enterprise and old Democratic states rights, new conservative "hard line" positions in the cold war, and uncertain gestures to imagery. He claimed he "tackled the civil rights issue head on" by mentioning it in every Southern speech. Yet his talks revealed no specific proposals to alleviate the grievances of Negroes. In North Carolina, for example, he said: "I also recognize that law alone, while necessary, is not the answer to the problems of human rights . . . that law is only as good as the will of the people to obey it. That is why it is the responsiblity . . . of those of us in positions of leadership . . . to . . . promote within the people in the states the desire and the will to keep the law and make progress in the solution of these difficult problems."

On the farm issue Nixon faced the problem of replacing an unpopular Benson program without repudiating Ike's Secretary of Agriculture. He proposed to take surplus acreage out of production, and consume more surplus wheat and corn, proposals not terribly different from Kennedy's. But, in a gesture toward Republican ideology, he also said farm programs should be controlled more by the farmers themselves and less in Washington. He did not say how that should be done.

Nixon's weakness on domestic affairs was a chronic Republican weakness. "I contended that the traditional American way has always been to rely on the free choices of millions of individuals," wrote Nixon, "and that the role of government must be limited to encouraging and stimulating private initiative and to creating the right climate for the exercise of freedom, with equal opportunity for all." But he rarely gave examples of what he meant. He made all kinds of statements about what the federal government should avoid. He had few suggestions what states, cities, or individuals might do to help solve public problems.

On foreign policy, Nixon spoke more specifically. If elected, he said he would ask Ike to send Lodge to Geneva to prod the stalled nuclear test ban negotiations. Should no agreement be reached by February 1, 1963, "I would order the resumption of underground testing." To an American Legion convention he recommended economic sanctions against Cuba, whose Premier Fidel Castro had chased out dictator Batista nearly two years before, and was now nationalizing American businesses.

Kennedy, meanwhile, had been forced to confront the old handbills, cartoons, and clandestine whispers that bedeviled Al Smith in 1928. Novelist James Michener, head of Citizens for Kennedy in Bucks Co., Pa., reported voluminous hate mail, "persuasive and fearfully poisonous." It warned against a Catholic takeover of schools, the press, and the government if Kennedy won. The source of most of this "literature," said Michener, was the local Protestant churches. "My minister warned us in church last Sunday," said one Bucks Co. woman, " that if we voted for John Kennedy we would live to see the day when Protestants were crucified in Levittown shopping center."

Like Al Smith, Kennedy planned to face the issue in a major speech late in the campaign. Early in September he was challenged by a group of Protestant ministers, among them the noted Dr. Norman Vincent Peale. Their statement raised the old question: Could a Catholic President be loyal to the United States? The Democratic candidate accepted an invitation to discuss the issue before the Greater Houston (Texas) Ministerial Association.

"I believe in an America where the separation of Church and State is absolute—where no Catholic prelate would tell the President (should he be a Catholic) how to act, and no Protestant minister would tell his parishioners for whom to vote," he told 300 mainly Baptist ministers. The skeptical audience gave him a warm hand. Not all were convinced, but he seemed earnest and candid; the skeptics went away respecting him. Moreover, films of the speech were shown on television across the country, so that, in effect, it became a nation-wide appeal for tolerance.

The issue did not stop there. It continued to feed into the campaign in a steady undercurrent. "Ministers preached politics publicly and churches distributed the most vicious electioneering materials," said James Michener, of his Bucks Co. area. Nixon, evidently unfamiliar with the lesson of 1928, said later Kennedy's associates "on every possible occasion . . . were pushing the religious issue, seeing that it stayed squarely in the center of the campaign, and even accusing me of deliberate religious bigotry." Protestant Republicans had been challenged to prove their lack of bias by voting Catholic. For himself, said Nixon, he refused to talk religion and would not allow his backers to either. As we shall see, religion probably hurt Kennedy more than it helped him.

Like Nixon, Kennedy repeatedly spanned the continent. He visited 44 states, gave about 120 major speeches, and at least 300 minor ones. He managed to cover 75,000 miles, mainly by jet. For example, he might start out from Maryland in the morning, speak in Maine, fly to San Francisco that afternoon, go on to Alaska, and touch down in Detroit less than 48 hours after setting out. Both candidates seemed to be everywhere at once. They planned their time to be seen by a maximum number of voters, and for the greatest TV and newspaper coverage. They campaigned this way for the same reason Bryan went whistle-stopping and McKinley took to the porch; they wanted to be where the votes were.

Kennedy used newspapers expertly. He enjoyed the company of reporters, welcoming them aboard his plane, glad to share his plans and ideas. Observed Stewart Alsop, "Kennedy was always ready with some small needling or self-deflating joke, and he had the engaging habit of receiving reporters in his underpants." It is not surprising Kennedy often got a better press than Nixon.

The real testing of the candidates, however, came in the "Great Debates." The television networks had long since noticed that the average political speech could never draw as many viewers as the show—any show—it replaced. Now the networks proposed something closer to drama, a face-to-face confrontation between the candidates. Fortunately, both Kennedy and Nixon saw advantages to the idea. If either had been President he probably would have turned it down. Under the circumstances, Kennedy had nothing to lose. He was less well-known than Nixon, who had been on the national stage for eight years. He was glad to give voters a chance to compare him side-byside with the Vice President. Nixon, on the other hand, had been a good college debater. His self-confidence was bolstered by memories of the Checkers speech and his argument with Khrushchev. On television Nixon hoped to show he had more experience, balance and judgment compared with Kennedy. He also saw the debates as a chance to make a pitch to the Eisenhower Democrats, who may have been thinking about going home to their own party.

Though Nixon wanted a single "sudden death" debate, and Kennedy wanted five or more, they agreed on four. Nixon asked that the fourth be on foreign policy, his strong area, figuring the audience would grow each time. As it turned out, more people saw the first debate—on domestic issues—than any other. Kennedy scored high with them. His 14 years in Congress made him well informed on labor, education and economic issues.

Kennedy spent the day of the first debate with his staff memorizing data on employment, growth, production, and civil rights. Arriving early at the studio, he looked tanned, well rested, and confident. Nixon, after addressing a hostile union group in the morning, closeted himself in a hotel room with his wife and refused to see anybody. His TV experts, who wanted to brief him on the stage setting, lights, and other details, were rebuffed. He had lost weight after a knee injury early in the campaign, and he seemed pale and uneasy before going on. To hide his thick beard an assistant applied a coat of "Lazy Shave." Rogers, Nixon's television adviser, asked for two tiny spotlights to shine into the Vice President's dark eye-wells; Nixon himself requested that no "reaction" shots be made when he was mopping sweat from his forehead. (One was. It did not help his image.) Despite these precautions, Nixon, on camera, looked gaunt, hollow-eyed and tired in contrast to the alert Kennedy.

Both men repeated the themes of their stump speeches in the first debate, but in more detail. The country could do better, said Kennedy. "I'm not satisfied when we have over nine billion dollars worth of food—some of it rotting—even though there is a hungry world, and even though four million Americans wait every month for a food package . . . If a Negro baby is born—and this is true also for Puerto Ricans and Mexicans in some of our cities—he has about one half as much chance to get through high school as a white baby . . . I don't want the talents of any American to go to waste . . . I think it's time America started moving again."

Nixon opened by agreeing with Kennedy. He rejected the Senator's claim that more federal action was needed, or that the Eisenhower administration had stood still. "We have built more schools in these seven and a half years than we built in the previous seven and a half[3] . . . We have developed more hydroelectric power . . . than was developed by any administration in history. Let us take hospitals. We find that more have been built in this administration . . . The same is true of highways . . ." He had "costed out the Democratic platform," said Nixon. It would run "a minimum of 13.2 billion dollars . . . to a maximum of 18 billion dollars a year more than we are presently spending." The GOP platform would cost only 4 to 4.9 billion dollars more.

---

3. Later a reporter asked Nixon how he could oppose federal aid to education and still take credit for building more schools. He replied he did not oppose federal money for school construction, only to raise teachers' salaries. The latter led to "federal control" of what was taught. Kennedy pointed out that when Nixon voted to break a Senate tie on a school aid bill—against the bill—the issue was whether to give money for schools to the states, period. The states would decide how to spend it.

In the brief exchange with reporters Kennedy's alert, rapid-fire replies tended to refute Republican claims he lacked maturity. The debate gave his campaign a great lift. His crowds, noted Theodore White, took a "quantum jump" in Ohio next day, and they "seethed with enthusiasm." James Michener reported enough checks flooded his Citizens-for-Kennedy headquarters to open four more offices in Bucks Co. Oddly enough, only television viewers believed Kennedy had got the better of the first debate. Radio listeners, unable to compare the physical appearance of the candidates, generally thought Nixon had won. In consequence, the Vice President decided his image needed an overhaul. "I went into the second debate," he wrote later, "determined to do my best to convey three basic impressions to the television audience—knowledge in depth of the subjects discussed, sincerity and confidence. If I succeeded in this, I felt my 'image' would take care of itself." This curious statement reflected all the Vice President's uncertainties, about issues, ideology, and party identity. Did a man act a debater's role like Hamlet? Nixon's attitude resembled the GOP's. The party, under Eisenhower, had tried "to convey" a picture of unity and harmony, when the reality was something different.

Again, in one of the middle debates, Nixon revealed the ambivalance that somehow transcended the man to symbolize his party. A reporter asked Kennedy whether he agreed ex-President Truman owed the GOP an apology for having said where he thought it could go. Kennedy smiled and remarked that at 76 Harry Truman was unlikely to modify his speech habits. When Nixon's turn came, he launched into a sermon on morality in the White House. "One thing I've noticed as I've traveled about the country are the tremendous number of children who come out to see the Presidential candidates," he said. "I see mothers holding their babies up so they can see a man who might be President . . . And I can only say that I'm very proud that President Eisenhower has restored dignity and decency, and, frankly, good language to the conduct of the Presidency . . . And I can only hope that, should I win this election, that I could approach President Eisenhower in maintaining the dignity of the office . . ."

The Republicans, Nixon seemed to say, were ahead in clean language. This appeal to imagery made reporters familiar with Ike's salty private vocabulary squirm. Yet Nixon made the statement, evidently in the belief it would (a) identify him with Ike, and (b) win votes. After the debate, the Vice President, unmindful of image, let loose some epithlets of his own over Kennedy's use of written notes, hastily cautioning newsmen these were "off the record."

About 100 million people saw one or more of the debates, surely the largest political audience on record. A least 31 opinion studies were performed by scholars trying to find out what the debates meant to voters and whether they had changed any minds. Every study gave Kennedy the edge in the first debate, and most Nixon in the third. The other two were considered toss-ups by some, Kennedy victories by others; in any case, the main impression was that Kennedy had "won." He had gained what he hoped to. Never again would youth or inexperience be charged against him with any effect.

Did the debates decide the election? Kennedy said he couldn't have won without them, and a Roper poll showed that 5 per cent, or about 3.4 millions voters, determined their ballots on the basis of the debates alone. Other pollsters, notably Samuel Lubell, felt the debates changed very few minds, not enough to throw the election one way or the other.

Nixon's hesitancy—perhaps faulty intuition would be a better description—cropped up repeatedly in other events. It was especially notable when the Reverend Martin Luther King, Jr., eminent Southern civil rights leader, was arrested late in October in an Atlanta department store with 52 others while waiting for restaurant service. The others were released, but King got four months at hard labor. The Justice Department in Washington quickly drafted statements in support of King's plea for release. Copies went to Eisenhower and Nixon for approval. No word came from either man.

At this crucial moment Nixon's strong civil rights stand at the convention seemed remote and somehow irrelevant. The moment had come to translate rhetoric into action. Nixon, perhaps fearing to lose the votes of those big crowds in Atlanta, hesitated. On his campaign train an unhappy E. Frederick Morrow, first Negro presidential assistant (to Ike), wrote out a telegram for Nixon to send to the mayor of Atlanta. The Vice President's press secretary, Morrow reported, "put the draft in his pocket to 'think about it.' " While he was thinking, Kennedy called Mrs. King on the phone and his brother Robert spoke to a Federal judge in Georgia; 24 hours later the minister was free.

Kennedy's intervention may have been shrewd politics, as some claim. Yet three Southern governors had advised him early in the campaign to lay off statements in support of Martin Luther King's movement. The idea to phone Mrs. King and express regrets originated with Harris Wofford, a young lawyer on Kennedy's staff. The Senator, receiving the suggestion in a Chicago motel, did not hesitate or consult anybody. He placed a long distance call to Atlanta and told Mrs. King he would do what he could. Perhaps the act was neither pure expediency nor pure conscience. Who, least of all Kennedy, could have predicted its consequences? Yet it was wholly consistent with Kennedy's platform, with his campaign, and with the direction in which his party had been moving—Southern wing to the contrary—for 20 years.

When King's father, also a Baptist minister who had come out for Nixon a few weeks earlier (on religious grounds,) heard about the call, he announced he had "a suitcase of votes" to take to Kennedy. It is a fact the Democratic candidate's great majorities in Negro wards, North and South, helped him win. In Illinois, for example, where he squeaked by with 9000 votes, more than a quarter million of his total came from Negroes.

Would Nixon have swung some of these votes if he had stuck to a strong civil rights position to the end? He would not have needed many Negro votes to give him the election. Nixon, caught in the vise of indecision, balancing Ike's South against the industrial North, came up with a typical GOP decision. He stayed on dead center. Thinking he might win Texas, Louisiana and North Carolina, he kept quiet, and lost all three anyway.

In the campaign's last weeks Nixon sensed the tide running against him, and, at last, turned to the nation's father image for help. A handful of days before election Ike agreed to speak at Pittsburgh and Cleveland and barnstorm the New York suburbs. He came in like a whirlwind, calling Kennedy "a player who knocks the team all season and then wants to be coach." He righteously asserted that "the White House is one place where we should not depend on on-the-job-training of the occupant." It is a great tribute to the Eisenhower image no one had the heart to point out he himself had no experience in government and no interest in politics when he became President eight years before.

Nixon called Ike's last minute appeals "the most hard-hitting political speeches" the President ever made. They came too late to do the GOP much good. Emmet Hughes thought Ike took too long to get "his dander up." Theodore White felt Eisenhower spent the campaign waiting for a call that seemed as if it would never come. If so, he did not wait alone. In New York the GOP's television staff also twiddled its thumbs on Vanderbilt Avenue. Then, 10 days before election, it got a rush call for a series of last minute programs: the Nixon rally in Cincinnati October 25; Ike's Pittsburgh speech October 29; and an Ike-Nixon-Lodge triple-header November 2 from New York. In the final week Nixon went on television nightly at 7 p.m. (EDT) for 15 minutes. The day before election he appeared with Ginger Rogers and other stars in a four-hour telethon from Detroit.

In the waning days the Vice President reeled off a series of promises: a manned flight around the moon in the years 1966-69;

a summit conference with Khrushchev; a personal tour of Eastern Europe to "carry the message of freedom into the Communist world." When none of these aroused any frenzy, he proposed, the day before election, to send Ike to Eastern Europe and invite satellite leaders to the United States in return. Eisenhower suggested Herbert Hoover and Harry Truman join him to make a truly non-partisan mission. "It's a little late now for such a thing," Truman said mildly. "If it were going to be done, it should have been done seven years ago before things started going to pot."

In that frantic last week Nixon also made a 7000-mile jet trip to Alaska and back to fulfill his 50-state pledge. He had flown more than 65,000 miles, visited 200 cities, and given at least 150 major speeches. Yet the climax of the campaign was a jumble of unplanned speeches, telecasts, and expansive pledges. While Nixon worked Alaska (3 electoral votes) Kennedy was pounding the sidewalks of New York (45 electoral votes).

"I have always felt that above everything else a man must be himself in a political campaign," wrote Richard Nixon in *Six Crises*. "He must never try to be or do something which is not natural for him. Whenever he does, he gets out of character and loses the quality that is essential for political success—sincerity and credibility." Was Nixon "himself" in the 1960 campaign? Theodore White commented that the Nixon campaign had "neither philosophy nor structure to it, no whole picture either of the man or of the future he offered." In his rhetoric "one could perceive neither . . . any shape or history, any sense of the stream of time or flow of forces by which America had come to this point in history and might move on." Yet these shortcomings were not the man's alone. His indecision and rootlessness lay in the conflicts of the GOP's past. The same qualities that marred his campaign made him the great compromise candidate of 1960. Liberal and conservative Republicans accepted him because he was neither.

When it came time to evoke history, Kennedy appealed to the shades of Wilson, Roosevelt and Truman. Nixon was left with

antecedents whose "image" had soiled. McKinley had no message
for the 20th century. Teddy Roosevelt had been the renegade his
party rejected. Scandal dogged Harding. Depression hung like
a shroud over Hoover. As for Landon, Dewey, and Willkie, Nixon
was not going to be labelled "me too" and consigned to purgatory
by the Old Guard caretakers of his party's past. He aspired to be a
healer, a harmonizer, a soother of old wounds. GOP history cast
Nixon in the role, but it left him without models. In the end he
was forced to imitate one of the most popular Americans of the
century, his boss, Dwight Eisenhower. Ike was one of the few
Presidents in whom the Republicans could take any pride of ownership. And the key to Eisenhower's popularity was the fact that he
was not a Republican at all.

So Nixon, in one sense, violated his own campaign rule and
stepped out of character. Having such uncomfortable alternatives,
he did the best he could and parodied Eisenhower. He accepted
Rockefeller's program but tried to make it more palatable to Goldwater, just as Ike had once made peace with Taft. He wooed the
South with platitudinous statements on goodwill and states' rights,
and became the first GOP candidate to campaign in Mississippi.
He asked people repeatedly to vote the man, not the party, thus
contradicting his role as party leader. Ike's unwillingness to give
moral support to the 1954 Supreme Court's desegregation decision
was perfectly mirrored by Nixon's reluctance to speak when Martin
Luther King was arrested. With the chips on the table Nixon, in
civil rights, stood pat, while Kennedy (to use Lyndon Johnson's
phrase) shoved in his whole stack.

In other words, Nixon tried to be non-controversial, a unifier
and pacifier like Ike had been. Even in this his political antecedents let him down. Dignity and aloofness had been the hallmark
of true Republican candidates back to Lincoln. Nixon's image did
not lend itself to exploitation the way Ike's had; furthermore, the
Vice President would not allow it. In consequence, he cut himself
off from the source of the best advice, support, and campaign

techniques his party had to offer. He kept his TV advisers off Madison Avenue for the sake of image, but even then he ignored them. He gave up his Plans Board too. "I suppose," said James Michener, "he was tricked by his advertising advisers into believing that what the American people wanted was a bland new father image, a man who never discussed unpleasant truths, a man who looked like a President."

Michener was wrong. Nixon never let his advisers get close enough to trick him. He was fooled by his own mis-reading of the Eisenhower image. Ike had promised to go to Korea, and Nixon, when the game seemed lost, offered to go to Eastern Europe, and at last, a parody of his own parody, to send Eisenhower there. Why? What did it mean in terms of the past or future? Ike, the military hero, going to Korea to stop a war was a potent symbol. But it was not the same thing as his bearing freedom's torch behind the Iron Curtain (as if the satellites might welcome the gesture). "If I'm elected," said Kennedy with curt logic, "I'm going to Washington, D. C., and get this country moving again."

Nixon's own perception of the campaign, measured against what he said and did, is startling. "I believe I spent too much time . . . on substance and too little on appearance," he wrote. "I paid too much attention to what I was going to say and to little on how I would look." Probably he was thinking of the first TV debate. If he spent "too much time" on substance, it could only have been the substance of dead-center, non-controversy, and vague ideologies from a party past that failed.

Kennedy operated within the framework of a viable tradition. He didn't need a computer or an ad man to tell him to mention Wilson, Roosevelt and Truman in every speech. These Democratic Presidents evoked a continuity of national purpose stretching back to the moment when the GOP, in rejecting TR, had turned its back on the future and made inevitable the Democratic rebirth.

This is not meant as a partisan comment but a simple statement of fact. In 1960 the GOP had not yet been able to resolve its internal problems sufficiently to make a dynamic, campaign based on tradition, consistent ideology, and past performance. The party of Lincoln didn't have to in 1860. The party of Nixon, Rockefeller, and Goldwater was unable to a century later, and appeared to be handicapped for the indefinite future. The GOP was unlikely to come up with another Eisenhower very soon. The only substitute would be a program with broad appeal both within the party and to the voters at large, a tall order for Barry Goldwater.

This much said, Nixon came very close to winning in 1960. A record 64.5 per cent of the eligible voters turned out. Among them Kennedy received only one-tenth of one per cent more votes than his opponent. He got 303 electoral votes to Nixon's 219, but the latter won more states—26 to 23. (Mississippi's unpledged electors went for Senator Harry Byrd.) Nixon appeared to do well, but he simply didn't get the votes where he needed them. In Alabama, Georgia, Mississippi, and South Carolina he ran even better than Eisenhower—but not well enough to win. It was a poor payoff on his civil rights strategy to reduce the Democratic margins in the South but lose the electoral votes anyway. Kennedy won his pluralities where they counted—in New York, Pennsylvania, Illinois, Michigan, Minnesota, Massachusetts, and Texas.

The reason Nixon almost surely appeared to do better than his campaign warranted was the impact of Kennedy's religion. Most analysts suggest, if anything, his Catholicism cost the Democratic candidate more votes than it gained him. Catholics tended to vote for Kennedy and Protestants for Nixon; however Catholics, before Eisenhower, had been traditional Democrats anyway. (Still one must remember that more than half of Kennedy's votes came from white Protestants in all regions.) The most fascinating statistic that bears on religion got little publicity after the campaign. At least 250,000 people cast ballots for other offices, but not for President. It is believed most of them were natural Democrats who could not bring themselves to vote either Republican or Catholic and so, locked in a dilemma, voted neither. And Kennedy's national plurality was less than 120,000 votes.

No President in history made more campaign promises than John F. Kennedy. His pledges tended to be in the bread-and-butter tradition of the New Deal and the Fair Deal. Kennedy had spent 14 years in Congress, and had an exact feel for what Presidents could or could not get if they tried; he was sure Eisenhower had asked for and gotten too little. With Wilson, Roosevelt and Truman, he believed the President should lead Congress and prod it. He vowed, if elected, to do that and more. "He was impatient," wrote historian Allan Nevins, "as he repeatedly said, with a society which used hardly half its industrial capacity, which let children go hungry while food surpluses piled up, which allowed Russia to produce twice as many scientists and technologists, and which grossly neglected its natural resources."

Kennedy made (by *Congressional Quarterly's* count) 220 campaign promises: 54 in foreign policy; 15 on national security; 41 in labor and welfare; 21 in agriculture; 24 on national resources; 14 for commerce; 16 on economic policy; and 35 on general government and judiciary matters. No power bloc escaped Kennedy's notice. Business and labor alike could find comfort in what he pledged. But he also promised on behalf of the amorphous groups like consumers, and the poor whites of the Appalachian region, who had no powerful spokesman and could not be expected to deliver bloc votes.

Kennedy pledged in part because it was his party's habit; but perhaps the number and variety of his promises contained a very personal element too. As Tom Wicker, of the New York *Times* observed, Kennedy enjoyed politics not because he thought he could improve the planet but because, commited to public service, he found it exhilarating to try. "Kennedy seemed sometimes to think of himself as taking the first steps he so often urged upon the country and the world," wrote Wicker. "He would use politics, he would propose a program, not with much hope for either, but to raise a question, to start someone thinking, to bring a matter into whatever light there was."

To list all of Kennedy's promises would take a book. Their wide range and concreteness may be judged from this sampling:

—not to be the first to start atmospheric nuclear tests;

—bring more African students to the United States;

—set up an arms control research institute;

—increase the nation's "nuclear retaliatory power";

—encourage South American land reform;

—call a conference on automation;

—strengthen ties with Poland;

—establish a Peace Corps;

—sign an executive order against housing discrimination;

—give federal medical aid to older people;

—extend social security laws;

—appropriate money for school construction and higher teachers' salaries;

—make loans to medical students;

—expand the Food for Peace program;

—protect farm cooperatives from "punitive taxation";

—reduce wheat production below consumption levels;

—fight water pollution;

—expand urban renewal programs under a new cabinet officer;

—reduce interest rates and ease credit;

—fight for stable prices by bringing pressure on management and labor both;

—submit a conflict of interest code to Congress;

—make non-partisan Cabinet appointments;

—end racial discrimination in every area of federal authority.

The list seems endless. Attacking "unfinished business" was what Kennedy meant when he said he wanted to "get this country moving again." He had priorities, of course; and he found some promises easier made than kept, especially when he needed the help of Congress. In the privacy of his own mind, based on 14 years of experience, he knew too that a President was in an especially good spot to blame Congress for failures of legislation. He also had a good party precedent: Harry Truman's attacks on the "do-nothing 80th Congress."

But Kennedy seemed more inclined to conciliate Congress than to blame it, to start many things rather than try to force one or two momentous ones to quick conclusions. Studying the record of Kennedy's successes and failures, it seems fair to say he thought that, given enough time, he could do *something* about each of his pledges. In his two years, 10 months and two days as President, he struck out in many new directions.

"Seeing so much that needed to be done, "wrote Allan Nevins, "he urged upon his first Congress a program so large and varied that full execution was impossible. At the end of his White House years some of his best hopes were still unfulfilled, primarily because his urgent aims were so numerous, because his reach exceeded his grasp. But in how much, at the same time, he had succeeded!" He tried and failed to get bills on medical care for the aged and aid to education. The latter bill was lost, in fact, because the Catholic Kennedy adamantly refused to include Federal grants to Catholic schools, thus proving he could act precisely the way he told the ministers at Houston he would. He pushed Congress to set up a Department of Urban Affairs in the cabinet, and Congress refused, partly because of its rural orientation. At his death the civil rights bill was bogged down, the tax cut not yet passed.

But in each of these fields he made beginnings. He was the first President to assert civil rights included a moral dimension, and to say so repeatedly and in public, setting a precedent Johnson would soon follow. Conservatives accused him of pushing the federal government into areas where it didn't belong, of spending too much money, of interfering in business, of forcing civil rights. Liberals charged him with insufficient commitment to their aims, too, specifically that he didn't push hard enough on Medicare, that he let Senator Estes Kefauver down in his bill to regulate drugs, that he dallied too long on civil rights, and that he failed to "take his case to the people," in the manner of FDR and the fireside chat.

Yet, in starting so many things, Kennedy could claim one kind of success, especially in contrast to Eisenhower, who had aspired to little more than keeping the boat afloat. Most liberals, for example, overlooked Kennedy's quiet White House civil rights revolution which elevated the status of tens of thousands of Negroes in federal service. Despite GOP skepticism, the Peace Corps became popular and effective. The Cuban missile confrontation with Russia, and the nuclear test ban treaty that followed, probably marked a turning point in the cold war. Kennedy's first steps toward a more modern view on the federal economy—including a tax cut—turned out to stimulate business more than the preceding eight years of "business administration."

Kennedy never lost sight of where the votes were; but the Democratic majority was based on an ideology his party had been reiterating for more than 30 years—to do for people what they could not do for themselves. If the GOP charged him with "vote-grubbing," so be it. Republicans, too, were entitled to grub all the votes they could get; they could hardly blame their failures on Kennedy's opportunism. Citizens can give their votes, but they can also transfer them, as they did to Eisenhower in 1952. Kennedy was aware of "image" and the benefits to a President of a good press. Perhaps even more than Nixon he knew what it took to look good to the voters. Yet "image," in a politician, is not enough to keep people coming back for more. Roosevelt was loved by so many people because he delivered something they wanted and needed. No President, no candidate for President, can hope to support for very long a facade for its own sake.

In his acceptance speech Kennedy said he would campaign on a set of challenges, not a set of promises. In fact he did both. He urged citizens in his inaugural to ask what they could do for their country. His notable failure, perhaps, was in not providing specific programs to follow up on this compelling phrase. He gave young people a vision of service with the Peace Corps; he asked labor to scale down its wage demands, and made the steel companies hold the price line. But for the suburbanites, who symbolize the American norm in the ads and movies and on television, he had no specific tasks. Suppose, for example, he had pushed a voluntary program to get middle-class people to tutor slum children nights and weekends? The response, from bored people looking for something useful, might have been fantastic—much greater than to his less tangible appeals for them to acquiesce passively in foreign aid or urban renewal.

Kennedy, campaigning for President, stirred up the desires of a lot of people to serve; many remained willing, eager, and uncalled. This is part of the enormous tragedy of his murder November 22, 1963. Not only had he still to fulfill his Presidency, he left millions who had hoped through his leadership to fulfill themselves.

Perhaps when the real innovation of the Kennedy campaign is assessed it will not turn out to be the grandiose promises, or the Great Debates, or the resolution of the Catholic issue. Perhaps it will be the effort—not quite successful—to involve millions of citizens of this utterly complex and sometimes incomprehensible nation in a sense that they shared their own destiny. "Now the trumpet summons us again," he said in his inaugural, to "a call to bear the burden of a long twilight struggle . . . against the common enemies of man: tyranny, poverty, disease and war itself." The voice was not Kennedy's alone. In it could be heard faint echoes of Douglas, of Bryan, and of the President's mentors, Wilson, Roosevelt, Truman.

The Democrats in the 20th Century had broken new ground campaigning for President. And the next GOP President, if he were to be a politician and not merely an image, would have to do the same. Campaign techniques—the train, the radio, television, motorcades—resulted from a need candidates had to be heard.

Techniques did not shape issues, they only made possible their transmission to the people. It would take more than a handsome face, or a good format, to win elections in 1964 and beyond. The GOP, as of this writing, needed an alternative program to Kennedy-Johnson. That was a big order, almost as big as finding an alternative to the New Deal in the Roosevelt years. If Democrats had monopolized the Presidency in this century, it was no accident. We tend to forget that Republicans too once monopolized the office, and for good reasons.

The power balance was not likely to shift by coincidence. If Lyndon Johnson's party continued to deliver what most citizens wanted, citizens would return it to power. Bobby Baker may have been a scandal, but he was hardly a campaign issue. No Democratic candidate won the Presidency blasting the mistakes of the past. They did it by painting a mural of the future. This is what the GOP had done after the Civil War. Republicans stood for land, trade, growth, railroads, industry, and a potent nationalism in the 19th Century. And Democrats, after the Great Depression, symbolized food, jobs, welfare, opportunity and hope. Barry Goldwater's party might enlarge the art of campaigning in the 1960's but it couldn't hope to succeed until its leaders took a new reading of the nation's pulse and precribed a real alternative to Democratic progress.

BIBLIOGRAPHY

Below are listed some of the sources used in the writing of this book. I would like to single out for special note the Oral History Collection of Columbia University as a source of some of the first-hand acounts of events described herein.

Adams, Samuel Hopkins. *Incredible Era: The Life and Times of Warren Harding.* Boston, 1939.

Adams, Sherman. *Firsthand Report.* New York, 1961.

Albertson, Dean, ed. *Eisenhower As President.* New York, 1963.

Allen, Frederick Lewis. *Only Yesterday.* New York, 1931.

Bagby, Wesley M. *The Road to Normalcy: The Presidential Campaign and Election* of 1920.

Bendiner, Robert. *White House Fever.* New York, 1960.

Binkley, Wilfred E. *American Political Parties: Their Natural History.* New York, 1958 (3rd Revised).

Bishop, Joseph Bucklin. *Presidential Nominations and Elections.* New York, 1916.

Bristow, Joseph L. *Fraud and Politics at the Turn of the Century.* New York, 1952.

Brogan, D. W. *Politics in America.* New York, 1960 (Anchor Ed.)

Brown, John Mason. *Through These Men.* New York, 1956.

Brown, William Burlie. *The People's Choice: The Presidential Image in the Campaign Biography.* Baton Rouge, 1960.

Bryan, William Jennings. *The First Battle.* Chicago, 1896.

Bryce, James, *The American Commonwealth.* New York, 1959 (Capricorn Ed., 2 vols.)

Carter, John Franklin. *Power and Persuasion.* New York, 1960.

Cannon, James M., ed. *Politics, U.S.A.* Garden City, 1960.

Clemens, Cyril. *The Man From Missouri: A Biography of Harry S. Tru-Truman.* Webster Grove, Mo., 1945.

Cox, James M. *Journey Through My Years.* New York, 1946.

Coyle, David Cushman. *Ordeal of the Presidency.* Washington, 1960.

Croly, Herbert. *Marcus Alonzo Hanna.* New York, 1923.

David, Paul T., Ralph M. Goldman, Richard C. Bain. *The Politics of National Party Conventions.* Washington, 1960.

Davidson, John Wells, ed. *A Crossroads of Freedom: The 1912 Campaign Speeches of Wodrow Wilson.* New Haven, 1956.

Davis, Kenneth S. *A Prophet In His Own Country: Triumphs and Defeats of Adlai E. Stevenson.* New York, 1957.

Day, Donald, ed. *Will Rogers On How We Elect Our Presidents.* Boston, 1952.

Dunn, Arthur W. *From Harrison To Harding.* New York, 1922 (2 vols).

Elliott, Charles Winslow. *Winfield Scott: The Soldier and the Man.* New York, 1937.

Ernst, Morris L. and David Loth. *The People Know Best: The Ballots* vs. *the Polls.* Washington, 1949.

Farley, James A. *Behind The Ballots: The Personal History of a Politician.* New York, 1938.

Fite, Emerson David. *The Presidential Campaign of 1860.* New York, 1911.

Flynn, Edward J. *You're The Boss.* New York, 1947.

Freidel, Frank Burt. *Franklin D. Roosevelt.* Boston, 1952 (3 vols+)

Friedman, Murray. *Voyage Of A Liberal.* (Unpublished PhD dissertation on Wendell Willkie.) Washington, 1958.

Goldman, Eric F. *The Crucial Decade: America 1945-1955.* New York, 1956.

Gosnell, Harold F. *Champion Campaigner: Franklin D. Roosevelt.* New York, 1952.

Handlin, Oscar. *Al Smith And His America.* Boston, 1958.

Hayes, Melvin L. *Mr. Lincoln Runs For President.* New York, 1960.

Heckscher, August, ed. *The Politics Of Woodrow Wilson,* New York, 1956.

Hesseltine, William B. *Ulysses S. Grant, Politician.* New York, 1935.

Hicks, John D. *The Populist Revolt.* Minneapolis, 1931.

Hofstadter, Richard. *The American Political Tradition And The Men Who Made It.* New York, 1948.

Hoover, Herbert. *Memoirs.* New York, 1952 (vol. and the Great Depression)

Howland, Louis. *Stephen A. Douglas.* New York, 920.

Hoyt, Edwin Palmer. *Jumbos And Jackasses, A Popular History of the Political Wars.* New York, 1960.

Hughes, Emmet John. *The Ordeal Of Power: A Political Memoir of the Eisenhower Years.* New York, 1963.

Johnson, Walter. *1600 Pennsylvania Avenue.* Boston, 1960.

Kelley, Stanley, Jr. *Political Campaigning.* Washington, 1960.

Kelley, Stanley, Jr. *Professional Public Relations And Poitical Power.* Baltimore, 1956.

Kelly, Frank K. *The Fight For The White House: The Story of 1912.* New York, 1961.

Kennedy, John F. *The Speeches of John F. Kennedy.* United States Senate (vol. I). Washington, 1961.

Kennedy, John F. and Richard M. Nixon. *The Joint Appearances of John F. Kennedy and Richard M. Nixon.* United States Senate (vol III). Washington, 1961.

Knoles, George H. *The Presidential Campaign and Election of 1892.* Palo Alto, 1942.

Kohlsaat, H. H. *From McKinley To Harding.* New York, 1923.

Kraus, Sidney, ed. *The Great Debates: Background, Perspective, Effects.* Bloomington, 1962.

Leech, Margaret. *In The Days of McKinley,* New York, 1959.

Link, Arthur S. *Wilson: The Road to the White House.* Princeton, 1947.

Link, Arthur S. *Woodrow Wilson and the Progressive Era 1910-1917.* New York, 1954.

Lubell, Samuel. *The Future Of American Politics.* New York, 1955 (2nd Revised).

Lubell, Samuel. *Revolt Of The Moderates,* New York, 1956.

McClure, A. K. *Our Presidents And How We Make Them.* New York, 1900.

Martin, Joseph W. Jr., *My First Fifty Years In Politics.* New York, 1960.

Mayer, Martin. *Madison Avenue, U.S.A.* New York, 1958.

Mencken, Henry L. *On Politics: A Carnival of Buncombe.* New York, 1960.

Michelson, Charles. *The Ghost Talks.* New York, 1944.

Michener, James A. *Report Of The County Chairman.* New York, 1961.

Moley, Raymond. *After Seven Years.* New York, 1939.

Moore, Edward A. *A Catholic Runs For President.* New York, 1956.

Nixon, Richard M. *Six Crises.* Garden City, 1962.

Peel, Roy V. and Thomas Donnelly. *The 1928 Campaign: An Analysis.* New York, 1931.

Peel, Roy V. and Thomas Donnelly. *The 1932 Campaign: An Analysis.* New York, 1935.

Porter, Kirk and Donald Bruce Johnson. *National Party Platforms 1840-1956.* Urbana, 1956.

Redding, Jack. *Inside The Democratic Party.* Indianapolis, 1958.

Roosevelt, Franklin D. (Samuel Rosenman, ed.) *Public Papers And Addresses.* New York, 1938-41.

Sait, Edward McChesney. *American Parties And Elections*. New York, 1942 (3rd Revised).

Schlesinger, Arthur M. *The Crisis Of The Old Order*. Boston, 1957.

Sinclair, Andrew. *Prohibition, The Era of Excess*. Boston, 1962.

Smith, Alfred E. *Up To Now: An Autobiography*. New York, 1929.

Stanwood, Edward. *A History Of The Presidency*. Boston, 1916 (2 Vols.)

Steffens, Lincoln. *Autobiography*. New York, 1931.

Steinberg, Alfred. *The Man From Missouri: The Life and Times of Harry S. Truman*. New York, 1962.

Stevenson, Adlai E. *The Major Campaign Speeches Of Adlai E. Stevenson*. New York. 1953.

Stone, Irving. *They Also Ran: The Story of the Men who Were Defeated for the Presidency*. New York, 1943.

Sullivan, Mark. *Our Times: The United States 1900-1925*. New York, 1930 (6 vols).

Thane, Elswyth. *Potomac Squire*. New York, 1963.

Thomsom, Charles A. H. and Frances M. Shattuck. *The 1956 Presidential Campaign*. Washington 1960.

Tillett, Paul, ed. *Inside Politics: The National Conventions 1960*. Dobbs, Ferry, 1962.

Truman, Harry S. (M. B. Schnapper, ed.) *The Truman Program: Addresses and Messages by President Harry S. Truman*. Washington, 1949.

Truman, Harry S. *Years Of Trial And Hope 1946-1952* (Memoirs, Vol. III). Garden City, 1956.

Walworth, Arthur. *Woodrow Wilson, American Prophet*. New York, 1958.

Warner, Emily Smith. *The Happy Warrior, A Biography of my Father Alfred E. Smith*. New York, 1956.

Wecter, Dixon. *The Age Of The Great Depression 1929-1941*. New York, 1948.

White, Theodore. *The Making Of The President 1960*. New York, 1961.

White, William Allen. *Autobiography*. New York, 1946.

White, William Allen. *Masks In A Pageant*. New York, 1928.

INDEX